# WHEN OPPOSITES DANCE

Roy G. Williams & Terrence E. Deal

# When Opposites Dance

**BALANCING THE MANAGER AND LEADER WITHIN**

Davies-Black Publishing
Palo Alto, California

Published by Davies-Black Publishing, a division of CPP, Inc., 3803 East Bayshore Road, Palo Alto, CA 94303; 800-624-1765.

• *Special discounts on bulk quantities of Davies-Black books are available to corporations, professional associations, and other organizations. For details, contact the Director of Marketing and Sales at Davies-Black Publishing; 650-691-9123; fax 650-623-9271.*

Visit the Davies-Black Publishing Web site at www.daviesblack.com.

07 06 05 04 03    10 9 8 7 6 5 4 3 2 1
Printed in the United States of America

**Library of Congress Cataloging-in-Publication Data**
Williams, Roy G.
When opposites dance : balancing the manager and leader within /
Roy G. Williams and Terrence E. Deal
p. cm.
Includes bibliographical references and index.
ISBN 0-89106-179-7
1. Leadership. 2. Leadership and management. I. Title.
HD00.0 .L000 0000
000.0´000—dc21

2000000000

FIRST EDITION
First printing 2003

To Lee Bolman and Carl Jung

# Contents

# Introduction

We often speak of life as a journey. Asked to tell your life's story, you no doubt would describe the peaks and valleys, the highs and lows experienced along the way. Your personal odyssey would not be like ours nor like those of any of the people profiled in this book. Yet, in one sense, we're all on a common path that we hope leads to meaning: discovering who we are, appreciating fellow travelers, and understanding our purpose for living. As you begin reading, we hope you will embark on a self-reflective, life-changing experience.

We have divided the book into three parts to assist your passage. Part one, Discovering Your Opposite, focuses on who you are now. In chapter one, Balancing Precision and Passion, we introduce *management* and *leadership,* terms people often confuse. Chapter two, The Management-Leadership Model, helps you determine your particular style of management or leadership.

Part two, Examining Management-Leadership Profiles, serves as a mirror. As you view the styles of a diverse cross-section of men and women, you will discover various aspects of yourself. Chapter three focuses on the rationalist, chapter four on the politicist, chapter five on the humanist, and chapter six on the culturist. All the profiles represent aspects of your personality, but you will probably find that one reflects your dominant style more than the other three.

Part three, Challenging Your Reflection, encourages you to move from reflection to action. Chapter seven, Reflecting While Dancing, suggests that you are ready to develop into a more accomplished dancer, regardless of the situation on your current dance floor. As you return to the roots of your past, reflect on your early years, and contemplate your newly discovered future, you will learn to dance with your opposite in new ways.

As you read the brief overviews of our journeys and study in-depth accounts of the profiles of others, we urge you to draw your own conclusions, enjoy yourself, stay alert, and remember: this book is about you and your inner journey at work and at home. Life's answers are not out there. They're inside. The key is to un-lock the treasure trove:

> Legend has it that when the gods made the human race, they fell to arguing about where to put the answers to life so humans would have to search for them.
>
> One god said, "Let's put the answers on top of a moun-tain. They will never look for them there."
>
> "No," said the others. "They'll find them there right away."
>
> Another god said, "Let's put them in the center of the earth. They will never look for them there."
>
> "No," said the others. "They'll find them right away."
>
> Then another spoke. "Let's put them in the bottom of the sea. They will never look for them there."
>
> "No," said the others. "They'll find them right away."
> Silence fell. . . .
>
> After a while another god spoke. "We can put the answers to life within them. They will never look for them there."
> And so they did.

—Marie-Louise von Franz

# Prologue

Wherever we go in life, we encounter managers and leaders. In the family, we call them fathers and mothers; in school, we call them teachers; in corporations, CEOs; in sports, coaches; and in the military, generals. But what makes a father, mother, or teacher a manager or a leader? Are people managers if they attempt to organize and thereby control us? Are they leaders if they attempt to inspire and thereby motivate us? Are styles of managers and leaders so different that there is no meeting place? Or is it possible for management and leadership not only to bump against each other but to embrace and dance together harmoniously?

Regardless of your answers to these questions, forms and functions of managers and leaders can evoke a sense of ambiguity, if not outright confusion. Some say leadership is a function of management: Managers are capable of leading, if only they can generate trust and articulate a vision. Others say management is a function of leadership: Leaders are capable of managing, if only they can handle details and organize the efforts of diverse constituencies. Because of these differing perspectives, studies of management and leadership offer few, if any, suggestions for bringing the two together in a synergetic dance of opposites.

Our view is that managers and leaders must first become aware of their personal leanings and styles if they are to dance with their counterpart. And, then, managers and leaders must recognize issues inherent in each situation for which they are responsible. Despite the fact that no two situations are alike, each nevertheless calls for balance. Thus, we suggest management and leadership must engage in an ongoing dance on "situational floors" where circumstances are constantly changing. Our individual dances began on floors that appear to be worlds apart. Yet along our separate journeys we learned a common lesson: the importance of dancing with our opposite.

# ROY WILLIAMS' JOURNEY

In my early career, I served on the staffs of two very successful collegiate basketball programs. During this time I earned first a master's degree in education and then a doctorate. As a result of my associations with several outstanding coaches, some of whom went on to coach at the professional level, I began to formulate a number of hypotheses regarding their coaching styles.

Here's what I learned: Coaches may be grouped into two broad categories: manager-coaches and leader-coaches. Regardless of the competitive level—high school, collegiate, or professional—the manager-coach is a basketball technician. He or she concentrates on the "X's" and "O's," the symbols that represent the five defensive players and the five offensive players involved in a game. In a manager-coach's controlled, highly orchestrated system, players are assigned clearly delineated roles that allow little room for error. If they execute the game plan with machine-like precision, they usually win or, at least, control the tempo of the game.

The leader-coach is a player's coach. He or she recognizes that players, not coaches, win games. Leader-coaches would be the first to tell you that their success stems from having more talented players than their opponents, not from manipulating the X's and O's more efficiently. They keep their individual egos under control and sell their superstars on doing the same. Players are empowered to utilize individual talents while contributing to the team. Giving players freedom, as opposed to plugging them into a predetermined system, is the key to the leader-coach's success.

Although both types of coaches experience success, I believe the leader-coach is more effective in the long run. Why? It's all about ego and winning. The manager-coach believes he or she wins games; hence his or her ego tends to be larger than the collective ego of the players. The leader-coach, on the other hand, believes players win games; hence his or her ego tends to be smaller than the collective ego of the players. As a coach, I learned that empowering players was far more effective than trying to control them. After all, coaches neither get the rebounds nor make the baskets that win games. Players do.

When I left the world of college basketball, I moved to Wall Street, where for twenty years I managed retail branches for two of the security industry's most prestigious firms. These firms employed thousands of retail salespeople (brokers) in offices across the country.

Through annual budgeting processes, I was responsible for submitting detailed plans that described how my offices would reach certain predetermined objectives. A large percentage of my management compensation was based on how successful I was in reaching these goals. As a result of this bottom-line focus, I constantly found myself facing a dilemma. My long-term people plans did not always translate into short-term financial goals.

Numbers were important, but so too was how those numbers were achieved. Coercing brokers to sell packaged products that resulted from investment banking relationships proved to be most distasteful. Security analysts often were paid huge bonuses for touting shares of a company for whom the firms served as investment bankers. When these strong-buy recommendations failed, retail brokers were left without supports as they attempted to console distraught clients who had trusted them.

Because my offices tended to be overled and undermanaged, I was often at odds with the higher-ups. I focused on people as opposed to results and, more often than not, succeeded. Notwithstanding, the nagging tension between developing people and pushing product remained. This ongoing conflict led to my ultimate resignation. I returned to academia, the place where I had begun my journey as a young man.

Upon completing my second doctorate at Vanderbilt University, I became an adjunct professor and taught two courses: "Understanding Organizations" and "Leadership." As both student and professor, I experienced a similar conflict to the one I encountered on Wall Street; it was just cloaked in different terminology. The dilemma our nation's institutions of higher learning grapple with is whether research is more important than teaching. Many parents pay hefty tuition fees for their sons and daughters to learn from the best professors at a particular school, only to learn that their courses are being taught by teaching assistants. Why is one thing promised and another delivered? Again I found myself wrestling with a familiar tension between people, research and teaching.

At many schools, research is the primary concern of professors. Students, a distant secondary concern, become lost in the academic shuffle. I have experienced many more overly managed classrooms than classrooms in which real teaching occurs. If I had to count the number of professors who fit the research, or management, side of the continuum versus those who fall on the teaching, or leadership, side, I would estimate, conservatively, a ratio of four to one. This annoyed me and continues to do so. Why can't research and teaching, management and leadership, achieve a better balance in higher education?

In *The Heart Aroused,* David Whyte describes my frustration with the tension generated by these opposites: "The 'mansion' of our soul is a poor hovel inhabited only by a fierce, heartless man guarding the entrance and a powerless woman locked in the cellar" (1994, p. 195). What Whyte is saying is that over time the "rational" exchanges between organization and individual leave a divided psyche. The masculine rational dimension has forced the feminine relational dimension into the cellar, into the unconscious.

As a result of my time at the university, I was forced to look inside and ask a tough question: Was I a "heartless man guarding the entrance" to the cellar of my soul, where a "powerless woman was locked"? Frankly, I was. Awareness of my feminine dimension began when I read *He, She,* and *We,* three intriguing books by Jungian analyst Robert Johnson. *He* stresses the importance of a man becoming aware of his Eve, and *She* stresses the importance of a woman becoming aware of her Adam. *We* focuses on integrating the two.

After reading Johnson's books, I plunged into Jung's voluminous works and became acquainted with masculine and feminine archetypes—animus (Adam) and anima (Eve). These archetypes encompass four types: thinking and sensing (more Adam-ish) and feeling and intuition (more Eve-ish). Then I began transposing

Bolman and Deal's four frames into Jung's types and archetypes and the subject of my dissertation was born. My purpose was to link the cognitive dimensions of management and leadership with their inner-psychic counterparts.

## TERRY DEAL'S JOURNEY

My career has not been a smooth, linear journey. I was a troubled kid—always in trouble and always at war with myself. I was a kid who thought he could fly. At the age of five, using a towel as a cape, I took off, only to hit the corner of a bench and rupture my spleen. I was also a kid who washed his money because I worried about germs. This struggle between risk taking and compulsion always seemed to get me in dutch. In fact, I was arrested and came close to becoming a ward of the California Youth Authority. Paradoxically, my first real job while in college was as a police officer. The juxtaposition of these contradictory beginnings was noted when I received an award from my alma mater, the University of La Verne. In presenting the award, the president commented that he had met few people who had ridden officially in both the front and the back of a police car. But through these divergent experiences, certain lessons in leadership were taking form: If you can walk in someone's shoes, you can understand them. And, when you have a badge that few respect and a gun you really don't want to use, you learn to work with people—even those you don't like.

Following my graduation from the University of La Verne, I spent five years as a junior high school teacher and a coach. My assignment was at one of the toughest schools in Pomona, California. There I learned another lesson: Every person, regardless of background, is a promise, and the job of a leader is to help him or her deliver. After Pomona, I moved to a high school in Pacific Grove, California, where I served as a teacher and then as principal of an experimental high school. The principalship revealed another vital lesson: Leadership and management always look easy until you are in command. This lesson was reinforced when I took the job as director of a residential school for older adolescents in

San Francisco. I realized again just how tough being the top dog is—even under the best of circumstances.

Licking my wounds, I assumed a faculty position at Stanford University, where I had earned a Ph.D. in between my teaching and administrative careers. That led to a study of schools as organizations, which revealed that symbols play a more powerful role than plans and policies in how organizations work. In other words: Efficient management is necessary, but it's effective leadership that drives the enterprise. Another lesson I learned at Stanford is that writing has two distinct functions. Penning prose is a passionate, creative process. Editing is a precise, technical exercise. For many writers, these two functions are at war during the writing process. Consciously alternating between the two produces readable, engaging work—a lesson that can be applied to leadership and management.

Later, as a Harvard professor, I followed my interest in myth, ritual, and ceremony—against the advice of many colleagues who warned about the dangers of studying fluff. That course of inquiry, however, led to the publication of *Corporate Cultures* (written with Allan Kennedy, a nuclear physicist and a McKinsey consultant), which became a best-seller. Leadership lesson: The fluff may be the real stuff. While at Harvard, I teamed up with Lee Bolman, almost my exact opposite. We managed to survive each other and our odd-couple dance produced the book *Reframing Organizations,* now a staple in most universities for those who study organizations. Our studies have documented that rationality is the big winner in efficient management but symbolism is at the heart of effective leadership. This lesson led to the publication of *Leading with Soul.*

In *Leading with Soul* (1995), Bolman and I introduced a character named Steve, a recently promoted young manager who is on a corporate treadmill. The grind is exacting an enormous emotional toll. Sensing his young protégé's condition, the company CEO encourages Steve to visit Maria, a gifted counselor. Following several visits with Maria, Steve's awareness level increases and he begins to understand the reason for his exhaustion. With Maria as his guide, Steve, like the mythic hero, enters the land of dark forests and deep lakes, symbols of the inner psychological terrain he must navigate to free himself from his psychic prison. Once he finds his soul, Steve begins to develop the relational, spiritual aspects of leadership that he needs to succeed. Writing this book was a deep dive for me. In the process, I found my own spiritual center. I also discovered another powerful lesson: Spirituality is at the heart of leadership, and true leadership lives in the hearts of leaders.

My Achilles' heel has always been my inadequate management ability. I am very poor with details and at observing important protocols. But my awareness of this potentially fatal shortcoming prompted me to hire Homa Aminmadani, a gifted manager. The two opposites—M*A*S*H's Radar and Colonel Potter—create a delightful balance.

At Vanderbilt University, I was Roy Williams' major professor, and I chaired his doctoral dissertation committee. Roy wrote a most unusual dissertation (completed in 1997). It fused two different ideas, conceptually synthesizing the four frames of Bolman and Deal and the four functions of Carl Jung. His dissertation forms the core of this book.

## THE CULMINATION OF OUR EXPERIENCES

It is clear from our backgrounds that we have both had our share of inner struggles with what appeared to be the opposing forces of management (precision) and leadership (passion). Both of us experienced successful careers—but not without a lot of stress and uncertainty. If only we had  known then what we know now, we would have had easier lives and probably enjoyed even more success. But now we know that awareness and acceptance of the tension between management and leadership allows us to find our balance, to be more creative, to dance with our opposite. This book aims to make our lessons available to you now, in the hope that you won't have to learn as many lessons through hindsight as we did.

# Acknowledgments

Each year the Academy of Motion Picture Arts and Sciences presents Oscars to those worthy of exceptional recognition. As a recipient receives the award, he or she makes a brief acceptance speech, acknowledging all those behind the scenes whose support made it happen. So, too, there is a cast of characters whose support made this book possible.

Chris Ousley, our artist, is responsible for the artwork. As you will see, he has an uncanny knack for capturing a person's character in a caricature.

The staff at Davies-Black performed above and beyond the call of duty. Connie Kallback, acquisitions editor, spent an extraordinary amount of time shaping the book to fit a Davies-Black audience. Both her feedback and her support were invaluable. Jill Anderson-Wilson, managing editor, was enormously generous with her time and advice. Laura Ackerman-Shaw helped with the graphics. Laura Simonds provided counsel on the marketing details.

Much of the book is based on secondary sources. However, several people made themselves available for interviews: Dan Reed, author of *The American Eagle* and airlines writer for *USA Today*; Tom Plaskett, former chairman of Pan American, who worked with Robert Crandall at American and Frank Lorenzo at Texas International; Jana Lewis, former regional marketing director for Southwest Airlines; Beverly Keel, writer for *Business Nashville*; Erwin Hargrove, political science professor at Vanderbilt University; and Bill Phillips, former White House aide to Presidents Ronald Reagan and George Bush.

The authors participated in Southwest's annual Culture Day in Dallas, Texas. Managers and leaders from organizations across the country were in attendance.

Homa Aminmadani, who serves as an excellent Radar to Deal's Colonel Potter (remember M*A*S*H?) was of great help on the logistics.

On the home front, Julia Williams, as a manager Roy's opposite, served in multiple capacities throughout the project: editor, expounder, and encourager, and, more important, Roy's partner in the dance of life. Dr. Sandra Deal served as a loving source of support. A clinical psychologist, she had her hands full with her husband over the course of the book's development. Their dance has lasted thirty years.

The intellectual foundations of our work rest on the shoulders of two individuals: Lee Bolman, whose work with Deal created the four frames, and Carl Jung, whose groundbreaking efforts form the intellectual foundation for the *Myers-Briggs Type Indicator®* personality inventory. It is to these two scholars we dedicate the book.

# PART 1

# Discovering Your Opposite

*How effective you are in embracing your opposite
determines how harmoniously
you dance personally and professionally.*

# CHAPTER 1

# Balancing Precision and Passion

Precision and passion, two sides of an apparent dichotomy, pose a compelling dilemma. Does sound management (represented by precision, logic, and thoughtful analysis) produce desired results? Or is productivity a function of inspired leadership (represented by passion, enthusiasm, and spirit)? Clearly, we need both. The right balance is dictated by the prevailing set of circumstances. Three American military campaigns illustrate the importance of management-leadership equilibrium.

On April 17, 1961, Brigade 2506 landed at Cuba's Bay of Pigs. The brigade consisted of Cuban exiles committed to overthrowing Castro and the Communist regime that ruled their homeland. As one volunteer put it, "It was my turn to do something for Cuba. Probably the purest thing I have ever done in my life was to make the decision to go" (Triay 2001, p. 7). Unfortunately, their deep resolve ended in a total rout. Of the 1,500 passionate commandos who stormed ashore, most were captured or killed by Castro's militia. Political intrigue and logistical mistakes destroyed their noble undertaking.

Fast-forward to the late 1960s and Vietnam, a war in which we monitored progress according to enemy body-count statistics. U.S. troops were well trained, equipped with the world's finest weaponry, and supported by awe-inspiring airpower. But too many soldiers did not know what they were fighting for or did not believe wholeheartedly in their assignment. A passionate, committed, and poorly equipped Viet Cong overwhelmed our technical superiority. Robert McNamara, the war's managerial architect, admitted years later that "we were wrong, terribly wrong."

Whereas the Bay of Pigs invasion was well led and poorly managed, the Vietnam War was overmanaged and poorly led. Fortunately, the U.S. military learns from its mistakes. Desert Storm is an example of how striking a balance between management and leadership can produce success. The superb management of the military campaign was matched by uncommon leadership from those in command as well as those in the teeth of battle. Logistical and political support given to frontline troops and pilots approached the miraculous. A well-thought-out battle plan laid out defined objectives. As one officer observed, "We have found that military options are too complicated to wing it." Critical supplies—fuel, food, and ammunition—reached troops on time and intact. Equally striking was the strong leadership that resulted in committed and motivated troops who believed in the cause for which they were fighting.

## THE NEED FOR BALANCE

Our awareness of the need for balance was never higher than following the crisis of September 11, 2001. A startled nation watched as fuel-laden airliners, piloted by terrorist hijackers, plowed into the World Trade Center towers. Moments later, another hijacked plane dove into the Pentagon and then yet another into a field in Pennsylvania, diverted from its target by the passengers.

The "Attack on America" brought a universal cry for leadership. Leaders know that words and deeds that satisfy only our heads seldom appease our hearts. Old Glory and patriotic songs— national symbols that speak to the soul—found renewed popularity. They represented shared values and principles all Americans could rally around to renew their spirits. Even so, in troubled times, kindred souls and brave hearts still need a dose of reason to balance the passion. An ongoing campaign against terrorism demands it.

Facilitating an enduring dance of opposites—rationality and spirituality—will sustain our nation with a sense of buoyancy and balance.

## Crises in the Workplace

Like warfare, business demands a balance between the coolness of analysis and the warmth of heart. Seldom has the need for productive tension between management and leadership been more evident. Many contemporary American businesspeople have not paid attention to this lack of synergy. As a result, many workplaces are out of balance.

Scores of companies have been overmanaged and underled, a point inferred by Jerry Useem in his article "Tyrants, Statesmen, and Destroyers: A Brief History of the CEO" (2002). Useem documents the evolution of the chief executive through several stages, caricaturing each style in the following manner: the Tyrant (John Patterson of National Cash Register), the Administrator (Alfred Sloan Jr. of General Motors), the Faceless CEO (Charles Wilson of General Electric), the Numbers Machine (Harold Genneen of International Telephone & Telegraph), the Statesman (Reginald Jones of General Electric), the Neutron Bomb (Jack Welch of GE), the Celebrity (Lee Iacocca of Chrysler Corp.), and the Destroyer (Al "Chainsaw" Dunlap of Sunbeam Corp.). As we move into the twenty-first century, Useem concludes that "the end of this disturbing trend is still not in sight" (p. 90).

Rapid turnover among corporate executives reflects this alarming trend. In "There's No Magic," Cheryl Einhorn cites a number of CEOs who appear to be failing in their attempts to turn around major U.S. corporations. "Chainsaw" Dunlop became the poster boy for rationally driven CEOs whose ruthless cost cutting to enhance the bottom line backfired. As Einhorn observed, Dunlop's "prowess might lie in financial engineering, not building a business" (2000, p. 26).

Dunlop was not alone. Joining him on the ever-expanding poster-boy billboard are the likes of Ken Lay, CEO of bankrupt

Enron; Bernie Ebbers, CEO of bankrupt WorldCom; Dennis Kozlowski, CEO of Tyco; Martha Stewart, CEO of Martha Stewart Inc.; and top executives of the disgraced accounting firm Arthur Andersen. Like Enron, WorldCom manipulated its financial statements, hiding billions in losses. Kozlowski was indicted for tax evasion. Stewart was accused of selling Imclone stock on insider information. And Arthur Andersen executives were suspected of aiding and abetting accounting cover-ups at several client firms. More dark images may yet appear on the list of "fallen messiahs."

"People simply can't trust corporate financial statements" (Valdmanis and Backover 2002, p. B1). Not only is Arthur Andersen out of business, but so too are many Wall Street analysts. Perhaps Charan and Colvin foresaw the growing tendency of corporate giants to place profits ahead of people. In their article "Why CEOs Fail," they suggest, "The motto of the successful CEO, worthy of inscription on his or her office wall, [should be] 'People first, strategy second'" (1999, p. 74).

We have arrived at a critical juncture in corporate America, one where the future of many firms hangs in the balance. Trust, the watchword of effective leadership, must be restored.

## The Collective Search for Leadership

The problem is that we're not sure where our new leaders will come from or if any will emerge at all. As organizations search for ways to rally visionary leaders while sustaining grounded managers, the business literature offers conflicting, and often misleading, messages. W. Edwards Deming, well known for his fourteen quality assurance points, eventually distilled the list to one crucial principle: It's all about spirit and meaning. Peter Senge, who coined the term *learning organization,* emphasizes that companies are living biological entities, not mechanical machines: "We need to think less like managers and more like biologists. . . . We need to realize that we're a part of nature rather than separate from nature" (in Webber 1999, p. 180). Capping these observations, management guru Peter Drucker confessed in *Forbes*:

Everything you've learned [about management] is wrong. . . .
One does not "manage" people, as previously assumed.
One leads them. The way one maximizes their performance
is by capitalizing on their strengths and their knowledge
rather than trying to force them into molds. (1998, p. 166)

Still other writers are bringing to light the forgotten art of leadership, best captured by Bennis and O'Toole: "Real leaders, in a phrase, move the human heart" (2000, p. 172). Unless the heart is moved, a heavy managerial hand can dampen a company's spirit. Recent management changes at Coca-Cola illustrate the point. Under the legendary Roberto Goizueta, a master of the human touch, "Coke reached new performance peaks. But things quickly eroded following Goizueta's untimely death. The board chose Douglas Ivester, second in command, to continue the course set by his boss. But members of the board failed to realize that Ivester was, in the best sense of the word, a number-cruncher supreme, an expert with financial instruments, balance sheet mechanics, and the like" (p. 172). Ivester was good with numbers but poor with people, and he was removed almost before he started. If, as Bennis and O'Toole surmise, the board had done its homework, "it would have quickly discovered that few Coke employees considered [Ivester] a leader" (p. 173).

But the absence of management produces its own perils. By most 2001 accounts, the Enron Corporation was flying high. Its top leaders, Ken Lay, Jeffrey Skilling, and Rebecca Mark, conveyed a robust vision of a company destined to become America's top corporation. Their zeal was proclaimed in boisterous company pep rallies and reinforced by an intense socialization pressure called "Enronizing." Roberts and Thomas concluded, "Anybody who did not embrace the elbows-out culture 'didn't get it.' They were 'damaged goods' and 'shipwrecks,' likely to be fired by their bosses at blistering annual job reviews known as rank-and-yank sessions" (2002, p. 26).

Clearly, at Enron passions were running high. But where were the management controls? Who was looking out for financial realities? Even with the stock dropping and rumors of demise running rampant, Lay and Skilling were pumping up the troops at motivational events. The Enron example clearly shows the dangers of passion overriding precision.

To conclude that either leadership or management is the key to business success begs the critical question. The real error stems from a long-standing tendency to be victimized by either-or thinking. As seen in the cases of Coca-Cola and Enron, we champion either management or leadership, favor left brain or right brain, choose rationality or spirituality. In our view, this sort of dichotomous thinking got us into trouble in the twentieth century. It poses even greater dangers in years ahead. The complex, knotty issues of today are not going to evaporate tomorrow. Rather, they will grow in complexity and volatility. To succeed, organizations need to develop a new brand of manager-leader; we crave people who have both feet on the ground as well as a lofty vision of the future. That's not a bad agenda item for the new millennium. But what are the probabilities that reach and grasp will coincide?

# DEVELOPING LEADERSHIP

Catalog offerings of the nation's top-twenty business schools reveal an overwhelmingly skewed ratio of management courses to leadership courses. Even classes dealing with the human dimension carry titles such as "Management of Human Resources." Harvard, among other schools, is taking steps to adjust this imbalance. Recently the "West Point of capitalism" adjusted its focus to include leadership and its "synonymous partner," entrepreneurship (Leonhardt 2000, p. E1).

To be sure, companies are spending millions of dollars to develop their human capital. But a sizable number of these dollars are still directed at teaching management skills: strategic planning, supervision, decision making, evaluation, and financial prowess. As one Harvard professor observed, "90 percent of the corporate training in this country emphasizes management rather than leadership. The 10 percent devoted to leadership is not done very well."

The same criticism can be leveled at university training efforts. First-year students, previously required to enroll in general management at Harvard, must now take "The Entrepreneurial Manager." Harvard realizes it must restructure its curriculum to include "the study of entrepreneurial ventures, be they dot-com start-ups or divisions of large companies trying to act like small companies" (Leonhardt 2000, p. E1).

But will restructuring curricula at the nation's business schools be enough? In a recent study, Stanford management scholar Jeffrey Pfeffer and doctoral candidate Christina Fong exposed glaring weaknesses in two fundamental areas by which business schools' effectiveness is measured: the correlation between grades and careers of their graduates; and the impact of faculty research on management practice. They concluded:

> Neither possessing an MBA degree nor grades earned in courses correlate with career success, results that question the effectiveness of schools in preparing their students. And, there is little evidence that business school research is influential on management practice, calling into question the professional relevance of management scholarship. (2002, p. 78)

Pfeffer and Fong found that consulting firms who hire and train people from other disciplines in the fundamentals of economics are as effective as business schools, not only in what their trainees learn but, more important, in how quickly they learn it. For example, hirees from law, medicine, and philosophy learn in three to four weeks what MBA students take two years to master (p. 81).

Consulting firms are not the only threat business schools face. Many organizations, including those in health care and education, are now taking very seriously the challenge to "grow their own." Organizations as diverse as General Electric, McDonald's, and Motorola are investing in local programs for developing human capital to both manage details and venture into new frontiers. We see the century ahead accentuating these emerging trends.

The September 11 terrorist attack on our nation dramatically underscores the point. In a *USA Today* article, Stephanie Armour says, "The terrorist attacks that took the lives of thousands of workers jolted people around the country into reevaluating choices they've made about their jobs, family, and career success" (2001, p. B1). Family and heart moved to the top of people's priorities, and career and wealth moved toward the bottom. Now "managers are concerned about the emotional welfare of their employees" (p. B1). A change in values often results from heightened awareness, which in turn involves being jolted from our complacency, yanked from our comfortable way of doing things.

## Change: An Imperative

Doing business in today's environment is not easy. In addition to dealing with terrorist acts, companies are being tossed to and fro by changing world markets, deregulated industries, and bewildering information-age technologies. To steer safely through these turbulent and unknown waters, executives often must let go of old ways. But knowing this and doing it are two different things. Executives are prone to choose tactics currently held in vogue by management gurus. After embracing, then discarding, total quality, executives reengineer, create learning organizations, and adopt matrix structures, hoping that integrating the vertical and horizontal dimensions of their organization will lead to cross-fertilization. Over and over, the cycle repeats itself. Heroic efforts continue to produce an inverse relationship between money spent and expectations realized.

Price tags for flirting with the latest fads are staggering. Researchers at Penn State estimate that business enterprises spend $100 billion annually to train employees. Of this figure, the researchers believe, more than 50 percent is wasted (Crainer 2000, p. 215). Another study concludes that $250 billion is spent each year on executive training. But are executives any wiser or more skilled as a result?

In *The Management Century,* Stuart Crainer describes the brief life cycle of a management fad:

[It] starts with academic discovery. The new idea is then formulated into a technique and published in an academic publication. It is then more widely promoted as a means of increasing productivity, reducing costs, or whatever is currently exercising managerial minds. Consultants then pick the idea up and tout it as the universal panacea. After practical attempts fail to deliver the impressive results promised, there is realization of how difficult it is to convert the bright idea into sustainable practice. Finally, there follows committed exploitation by a small number of companies. (2000, p. 185)

Using reengineering to illustrate his point, Crainer concludes that "the mistake of reengineering was not to tackle reengineering *management* first" (2000, p. 188). Reengineering organizations without first rewiring managers and leaders was doomed to fail. Real change requires both sound management and inspired leadership. When this dance of opposites occurs, change works; when it doesn't, the change quickly falls apart.

## Executive Coaching

Where is the balance between management and leadership that companies need to survive and thrive? As Ghoshal and Bartlett point out, many of today's companies focus more on strategy than on purpose, more on structure than on process, more on systems than on people (1997, ch. 11). As a result, organizations continually find themselves overmanaged and underled, an imbalance that too often leads to disaster. Is executive coaching an answer to CEOs' need to achieve a better balance?

In 2001, some 10,000 "coaches" rushed into organizations, many touting relatively simple solutions to what often are complex problems. The rapidly expanding business of executive coaching, expected to reach 50,000 practitioners in the next five years, is made up primarily of athletic coaches, former executives, psychologists, lawyers, and consultants. Their fees range from $1,500 to $15,000 per day (Berglas 2002, p. 89). One analyst concludes that many quick-fix coaches believe success lies "in 12 simple steps or seven effective habits" (p. 88), that is, in surface behavioral changes. Often "executive coaches model their interventions after those used by sports coaches, employing techniques that reject out of hand any introspective process" (p. 88).

As the search for management and leadership talent continues, many individuals are motivated to develop their own abilities. The sheer volume of articles, books, seminars, and conferences consumed by aspiring and experienced managers and leaders is overwhelming. Unfortunately, there is often no connection between what people consume and how they act. The tendency is to bounce from one fashionable idea to another, to master lists and tactics without reflection or soul searching. We are attracted to the easy, external quick fix, instead of accepting that a long-term, sometimes painful, inner dialogue provides a more promising pathway to both better management and more effective leadership. We attempt to fix others while ignoring the images reflected in our own management-leadership mirrors. In effect, we condemn the mote in our neighbor's eye while the beam remains in our own.

## DISCOVERING OUR OPPOSITES

One of the first steps toward changing our thoughts and deeds is becoming more conscious of how we think and act. Before we learn to dance with our opposite, we must first discover our potential inner partner. If we are male, for example, our opposite is our subconscious feminine side, and vice versa. Carl Jung emphasized that every man has his "Eve" and every woman her "Adam," or, in the words of Erik Erikson, a person may be thought of as "a universe of one" (Schön 1983, p. 16). Thus, a man will discover his humanist dance partner in the underdeveloped feeling and intuiting parts of himself, and a woman will discover her rational dance partner in her own underdeveloped areas of thinking and sensing.

Descartes concluded, "I think; therefore I am." Cognition helps us make sense of a complex, often unpredictable world. On a conscious level we all have our preferred patterns of thought. Some lean toward analysis and technical rationality. Others favor human support and participation. Still others see a world of scarce resources in which special interests exercise power to get what they want. On a deeper level, some of us yearn for a meaningful life and emphasize symbols as our source of inspiration and faith (Bolman and Deal 1997). These four cognitive orientations or styles of thought often oppose each other. For example, rationalists see humanists as weak; humanists accuse rationalists of detachment and rigidity. Culturists accuse politicists of being out for themselves; politicists depict culturists as idealists who lose themselves in a herd mentality. But the goal is to learn to dance with our opposite: Rationalists must become acquainted with their humanist side; politicists must discover the blessing of their culturist side, and so on.

## A Balanced Profile in Politics

How does such an awareness or integration occur? Sometimes dramatically changing circumstances demand it. Before the New York terrorist disaster, Rudy Giuliani was known as a no-nonsense manager whose tough policies had placed the city on firm financial pillars and reduced crime. After the disaster, he was widely heralded as "the World's Mayor," a compassionate, caring leader.

Why the transformation? As Giuliani himself described it, he moved from his head to his heart. As he called upon his inner core, he discovered his authentic concern for people and their needs. But Giuliani still maintains his tough, no-nonsense, style. He once told a reporter in an interview, "That's such a stupid question, it doesn't warrant an answer." Giuliani has learned to balance head and heart, male and female, management and leadership. But his new dance of opposites was triggered by a dramatic situation most of us would prefer to avoid at all costs.

We believe self-awareness can be achieved through other, less dramatic, means. People in managerial leadership roles can step back, do an inner inventory, find their strong suits and Achilles' heels, and identify their bright spots and shadows. Then they can learn to dance with inner opposites—or surround themselves with partners who can enhance the harmony externally.

We believe that a new century calls for an end to the continuing battle between management and leadership. Phil Jackson, coach of the Los Angeles Lakers, serves as an excellent example of someone who both manages and leads well. Jackson's ability to probe his inner depths is not only interesting but instructive as well.

## A Balanced Profile in Sports

Phil Jackson has led the Chicago Bulls and the Los Angeles Lakers to nine NBA titles, tying the record of legendary Red Auerbach of the Boston Celtics. In *Sacred Hoops,* he describes his approach to handling multimillionaires such as Michael Jordan and Shaquille O'Neal: "When I can be truly present with impartial, open awareness, I get a much better feel for the player's concerns than when I try to impose my own agenda" (1995, pp. 67–68). Such "impartial awareness" is also the key to Jackson's healing of his own internal "split between feminine and masculine, heart and mind" (p. 67). In other words, Jackson's balanced management and leadership orientation helps him deal with his players in an open manner. They then express themselves in the quasi-structured "triangle offense" Jackson's teams employ. Rather than fostering what theologian Martin Buber terms "I-It" relationships (in Frattaroli 2001, pp. 12, 145, 155) with players, in which he manipulates players as objects, Jackson fosters what Buber terms "I-Thou" relationships, in which he and his players participate in team goals. Consequently, Jackson, in our view, embodies virtues of a sophisticated approach to the management-leadership dilemma: finding a paradoxical balance between what historically have been competing polarities.

How do we get there? In the next chapter, we articulate the conceptual roots of the managerial-leadership equation and offer a model to help people find where they fit on a dynamic continuum, always in flux as situations change. The key is to become aware of your strengths, your leanings, and your deficits. Then you can either begin to expand your horizons, yielding a more complex and productive inner dialogue, or you can seek out your opposite and begin to dance. The form that the desired harmony takes will be dictated by the corporate context in which you work. Finding the right balance will enhance your career and, over time, help you contribute to a better corporate performance. In this way, you can help avoid the calamities of the Enrons, WorldComs, and Arthur Andersens of the world.

# The Management-
# Leadership Model

Too many managers and leaders are trapped in a state of mindless-
ness, held in place by rigid categorizing and imprisoned by unexamined mind-sets. They are always busy, if not overwhelmed, and
as a result, they make decisions and take action without thoughtful
reflection. This often results in mistakes, without much learning
taking place. If we don't heed the lessons of our errors, we are likely
to repeat them. The same is true of our successes. If we don't recognize why we succeeded, what are the chances we can do it again?

Ellen Langer (1990) describes an alternative: the state of mindfulness, the ability to be on the dance floor and in the balcony at the
same time—the place from which we can create new categories and
entertain novel ideas to fit unfamiliar situations. Mindfulness offers
an opportunity for reflection, which then leads to greater awareness. It is not that we don't strive to achieve this state of perpetual
acuteness: We read books. We take courses. We find mentors. We
look for exemplars, either good or bad. But somehow our reach always seems to exceed our grasp, and we keep stumbling and grop-
ing through life at work.

## A REFLECTIVE MODEL

Helping you discover where you are and where you need to go
along the management-leadership path is this book's primary aim.

How does this discovery come about? Through identifying with the profiles we present, you will understand the styles they reflect. Through reflection, you can know yourself better, and you can recognize and appreciate others more. This is also the first step in shaping a better workplace.

Where do we start on the path to a heightened state of awareness? By doing something we do every day: looking in a mirror. In this chapter, we present a model that serves as a mirror. While viewing your reflection, you can ponder your strengths and weaknesses. We believe people ruminate best when they entertain multiple perspectives and observe exemplars who embody different ways of thinking and acting. Our model's theoretical approach is built on two popular sets of lenses: the *Myers-Briggs Type Indicator*® (MBTI®) personality inventory and Bolman and Deal's Cognitive Frames model.

## The MBTI® Personality Inventory

How do we measure up as managers and leaders? Hundreds of inventories and surveys claim to capture the essence of effective management and leadership. No instrument, however, has been more widely used in this regard than the MBTI personality inventory.

In effect, this instrument transposes the Jungian archetypes of animus (male) and anima (female) into four functions: Thinking, Sensing, Feeling, and Intuition. These are juxtaposed into letter pairs.

- T (Thinking) versus F (Feeling)
- S (Sensing) versus N (Intuition)

To these sets of opposing functions, the MBTI instrument adds two others.

- E (Extraversion) versus I (Introversion)
- J (Judging) versus P (Perceiving)

These four paired sets yield four-letter individual profiles. The classic ESTJ, for example, is extraverted, concrete, rational, and decisive. The polar opposite, INFP, is inwardly focused, reflective, empathic, and open to ideas. The MBTI inventory articulates fourteen additional possibilities, often shown in a sixteen-cell matrix.

Empirically, most males lean toward the ESTJ prototype. Women tend to favor the INFP. This brings us back to the original Jungian concept of the thinking, sensing male (animus) and the feeling, intuiting female (anima). For management, the dominant pattern is ST, and for leadership, NF. Regardless of the pattern, one should always "speak of the differentiation of functions, rather than of the I.Q. of a person;" that is, "the intelligence of the heart" is just as important as the intelligence of the mind (Von Franz 1993, p. 43).

## Cognitive Frames

Bolman and Deal's concept of *frames* is anchored in organizational behavior and cognitive psychology. The authors distilled ideas from the four disciplines listed below. The logic unique to each frame creates a perceptual lens through which leaders and managers read complex situations and choose a course of action.

- **Psychology (human resources)**
  Human resources–oriented leaders emphasize human needs and work to build a people-centered climate. When looking through this lens, the leader's concern is that people's needs are being as well served as the organization's needs.

- **Sociology (structural)**
  Structurally grounded managers focus on results, clarity, and accountability. Managers not getting the desired results often reorganize the company, believing that a new structure will help clarify and accomplish the original goals.

- **Political Science (political)**
  Politically attuned managers mobilize power by rallying groups with different interests around a shared agenda. Managers looking through the political lens are searching for power that will let them control limited resources and wield requisite influence.

- **Anthropology (symbolic)**
  Leaders with symbolic leanings rely on charisma and inspiration to shape a cohesive culture that gives work purpose and meaning. Symbolic leaders emphasize symbols, rituals, and special events that reinforce the culture they are trying to shape.

## THE MANAGEMENT-LEADERSHIP MODEL

We have combined these two traditions—the MBTI personality inventory and Cognitive Frames—into a management-leadership model intended to function as a mirror. Notice that on the left side of Figure 1, The Management-Leadership Model, are the Jungian functions of Thinking and Sensing portrayed as the rationalist (advocating structural assumptions) and the politicist (embracing a power perspective). These orientations form the stuff of management, a more masculine, left-brain orientation.

The model's right side includes the Jungian functions of Feeling and Intuition, portrayed as the humanist (championing human resource logic) and the culturist (thinking and acting symbolically). These orientations form the basis of leadership, a more feminine, right-brain orientation.

At the circle's top and bottom, the left and right sides are integrated into the concept of a synergist, who is capable of assuming any orientation a situation demands, and an androgynist, who is comfortable with both male and female impulses.

For reflection purposes, these different orientations or categories should not be seen as discrete or tightly defined. We arrayed them on a horizontal continuum. You can begin on the leadership

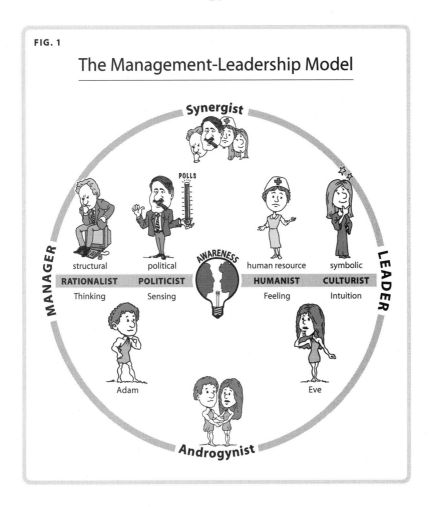

FIG. 1

# The Management-Leadership Model

side and consider your management options or vice versa. Before you begin, pay particular attention to the model's centerpiece: a light bulb symbolizing awareness. In the light bulb appear silhouettes of a man and woman "paying attention" to each other. The brighter the light bulb shines, the more aware the man becomes of his opposite, and the more aware the woman becomes of hers. Thus active awareness may be thought of as paying attention, and, in its essence, "attention is an act of connection" (Cameron 1992, p. 53). That is, when you pay attention to what you think, sense, feel, or intuit, your heightened awareness turns into a channel through which you and the object connect.

Occupying the central position in the model, awareness is the key to dancing with your opposite. For that reason, your first step is to find your comfort zone on the continuum. Then you move out of it to embrace your opposite on the other side, paying attention to the importance of maintaining a *balanced* relationship with it.

By balance, we do not necessarily mean a fifty-fifty split. Circumstances play a major role in determining the right mix of leadership and management. New York's Rudy Giuliani, Enron's Ken Lay, and WorldCom's Bernie Ebbers found themselves in situations that called for the ability to balance management and leadership. Because Giuliani recognized the catastrophic circumstances of September 11, 2001, he responded immediately by donning the hat of leadership. Ultimately, he successfully led New Yorkers through their worst nightmare. Because they refused to recognize the rapidly escalating financial crises engulfing their companies, Lay and Ebbers continued to manage as Enron and WorldCom spiraled out of control. Though their circumstances called for leadership, it was nowhere to be found.

As Lay and Ebbers sadly learned, life in organizations is not only chaotic but paradoxical as well. This makes it hard to determine exactly what is happening and what is the right action to take. But knowing your preferred style, your opposite, and your options is an important first step. Finding the right balance is the key to a successful career in which either-or thinking is replaced with reflection, the key to finding balance on the management-leadership continuum.

## THE DISCOVERY TOOL

To assist you in determining where you fit in the model, we developed the Management-Leadership Continuum Locator, a heuristic tool to stimulate self-reflection, the first step in balancing your internal manager and leader. There are two approaches to using the locator. If you tend to take a more objective approach to gathering information (using your senses), you may choose to complete the survey first and then move on to the profile chapters. If you prefer a more subjective approach (using your intuition), you may elect to read the profile chapters first and then complete the survey. Your choice says something about you, something we believe you will figure out in your journey through the book.

Completing the survey takes less than fifteen minutes. After you respond to items 1 through 6, plot your scores. Then you will be ready to determine your management-leadership profile.

## LEADERSHIP AND MANAGEMENT IN THE NEW MILLENNIUM

How we bring our opposites together and achieve a more harmonic balance is what the rest of this book is about. This means integrating our male and female aspects and thereby becoming more androgynous. It means embracing the styles of the rationalist, politicist, humanist, and culturist and thereby becoming a more complete manager-leader.

When you look at the apex and base of the model, you see the synergist and his or her counterpart, the androgynist. Synergists are self-actualized manager-leaders, people who have risen above the fray to integrate their four functions and their masculine and feminine dimensions. Maslow (1954) describes a similar process: "What had been considered in the past to be polarities or opposites or dichotomies were so only in unhealthy people. In healthy people, these dichotomies were resolved, the polarities disappeared, and many oppositions thought to be intrinsic merged and coalesced with each other to form unities. . . . Such findings have been reached for . . . masculine-feminine" (p. 233).

How does this dance of opposites occur? Maslow explains, "The age-old opposition between heart and head, reason and instinct . . . disappear[s] in healthy people where they become synergic rather than antagonists, and where conflict between them disappears" (p. 233). Conflict disappears when opposites dance to

# MANAGEMENT-LEADERSHIP CONTINUUM LOCATOR

**Directions:** This survey asks you to describe yourself as a manager and/or leader. Rank your answers to items 1 through 3 by placing a "4" in the blank next to the phrase that *best* describes your style, a "3" beside the next-best descriptor, then a "2", and finally a "1" next to the phrase that *least* describes your style. Each blank beside the letters A through D should contain a ranked number.

**1.** My strongest skills are

_2_ A. Thinking through problems

_3_ B. Caring for individuals

_4_ C. Analyzing situations

_1_ D. Appreciating human values

**2.** Most people would characterize me as being

_3_ A. Objective

_4_ B. Sensitive to others

_1_ C. Precise

_2_ D. Warmhearted

**3.** I enjoy people who are

_2_ A. Logical

_3_ B. Emotionally expressive

_1_ C. Rational

_4_ D. Compassionate

**Total:** _7_ A's  _10_ B's  _6_ C's  _7_ D's

**A's plus C's =** _13_ (R)
**B's plus D's =** _17_ (H)

*(continues)*

Follow the directions from the previous page to complete items 4 through 6.

**4.** I see myself as

___4___ A. Being imaginative

___2___ B. Paying attention to detail

___3___ C. Dreaming of possibilities

___1___ D. Requiring measurable results

**5.** My success stems from

___4___ A. Envisioning the future

___2___ B. Maintaining the status quo

___3___ C. Trusting my instincts

___1___ D. Setting rigid operating procedures

**6.** Most people see me as being

___4___ A. Conceptual

___2___ B. Factual

___3___ C. Theoretical

_____ D. Literal

**Total:** ___12___ A's ___6___ B's ___9___ C's ___3___ D's

**A's plus C's =** ___21___ **(C)**

**B's plus D's =** ___9___ **(P)**

(continues)

# Plotting Your Location

Place your first set of scores (R and H) as small *x*'s on the solid vertical lines under Rationalist and Humanist, respectively, and your second set of scores (C and P) on the dashed lines under Culturist and Politicist, respectively. Now connect your *x* scores. Does your personal continuum parallel the one at the bottom; that is, is it balanced, with equal numbers on the left and right?

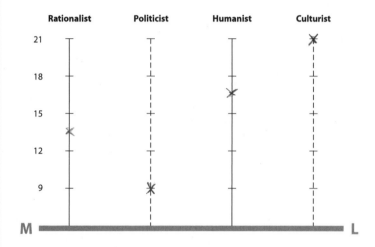

If your two highest scores are on the left side of the continuum under Rationalist and Politicist, you tend to be a Manager. If your two highest scores are on the right side of the continuum under Humanist and Culturist, you tend to be a Leader. If your two highest scores are split (one on each side of the continuum), your style reflects elements of managing and leading.

Becoming aware of your locations—both strengths and weaknesses—is the first step toward addressing your management-leadership style. Continual development of your two lesser functions facilitates integrating them with your two stronger functions. As a result of this ongoing process, you begin to see situations from a different perspective, as if you were viewing them from a balcony. Your enhanced level of awareness allows you to move up and down the continuum as only a balanced manager-leader can.

*(continues)*

# Understanding Your Location

**1. Rationalists:** *Thinking* is the dominant function of rationalists. Because they are ruled by their heads, rationalists analyze a situation on the merits of available empirical evidence. They tend to be logical and precise in their style, a result of their drive to obtain objective results. This explains why rationalists enjoy the company of people who, like themselves, take a reasoned approach to solving problems.

**2. Politicists:** *Sensing* is the dominant function of politicists. Politicists rely on their senses to navigate constantly changing political landscapes. Through the use of polls, they focus on measurable results. Because they must see and identify with the reality of their constituencies, politicists tend to be practical, factual, and literal. In other words, they rely on common sense.

**3. Humanists:** *Feeling* is the dominant function of humanists. Ruled by their hearts, humanists tend to reach decisions by filtering them through a personal values system. Being warmhearted and compassionate, humanists empathize with the needs of people. Their personable approach finds them enjoying people with caring attitudes.

**4. Culturists:** *Intuition* is the dominant function of culturists. Being imaginative, culturists tend to envision the possibilities in situations. When considering the future, they can be quite innovative. Under the influence of their intuition, culturists tend to rely on their hunches. Having active imaginations, culturists enjoy the company of people who take theoretical approaches to problems and their solutions.

*(continues)*

# Determining Your Balance

Now that you have completed the Management-Leadership Continuum Locator, you can pinpoint whether your dominant style places you on one side of the model or the other. Are you primarily a rationalist? A politicist? A humanist? Or a culturist? Are you on the left side or the right side? Remember, you are all four, but one reflects your dominant style better than the other three. Once you've identified your dominant style, you've taken the first step toward discovering your opposite and eventually learning to dance.

Let's look at the possibilities. If the locator determines that you, like Rudy Giuliani, are primarily a rationalist, you need to get in touch with your humanist dimension, as he did. Looking again at the model, you can see that your rationalist approach places you on the left side of the continuum, and the humanist, your opposite, is located on the right side. Like Guiliani, your task is getting to the other side, getting out of your head and into your heart, moving from the management side to the leadership side.

If the politicist is your dominant style, then your task is to learn to dance with your culturist dimension, again moving to the right side of the continuum. If your dominant style is the humanist, you need to learn to dance with your rationalist side. If your dominant style is the culturist, you should move toward your politicist leanings.

Recall, each of us typically favors one of the dimensions over the other three. There is nothing wrong with this; it simply proves we are individuals. Our dominant function is the primary means we use to adjust to our environment. Even so, when we step back and observe ourselves in the mirror, we can embrace more of our full potential.

the same music. When the Adams and Eves of men and women escape their psychic prisons, they are drawn to each other, uniting as androgynists. When we integrate our rational, political, human, and symbolic thinking, we find synergistic energy. Once you feel comfortable with these ideas, the next step involves a thorough and thoughtful self-analysis.

## REAL-LIFE EXAMPLES

Beginning in Chapter 3, we present our portraits of real-life examples of each style represented in the model. The choices are personalities we believe you can identify with.

### Airlines Reflect Capitalism

We chose the airline industry from which to select our examples because the airlines incorporate the primary components of a capitalistic enterprise. Airline companies are capital intensive in that they use expensive aircraft; they are technology intensive in that they rely on sophisticated flight and reservations systems; they are service intensive in that they transport the traveling public; and they are labor intensive in that they are heavily unionized. One writer uses an assembly line metaphor to describe how these factors create the end product: "a trip by an individual" whose needs differ from those of other travelers. Airlines produce roughly 700 million individual "products" each year. Unlike a car manufacturing assembly line that can be stopped by the jerk of a cord, an airline is subject to circumstances beyond its control: inclement weather, mechanical failures, in-flight passenger emergencies, and terrorist hijackings (Reed 2002, p. B3).

Since its deregulation in 1978, few industries have experienced as much turmoil and transformation as the airline industry. In the aftermath of 9-11, the turbulence has reached a crescendo. Carriers teeter on the brink of bankruptcy, and others are forced to restructure to survive. Fewer fliers, tighter airport security, and escalating costs (particularly labor) are but a few of the problems facing leadership. Even venerable Southwest is encountering unanticipated

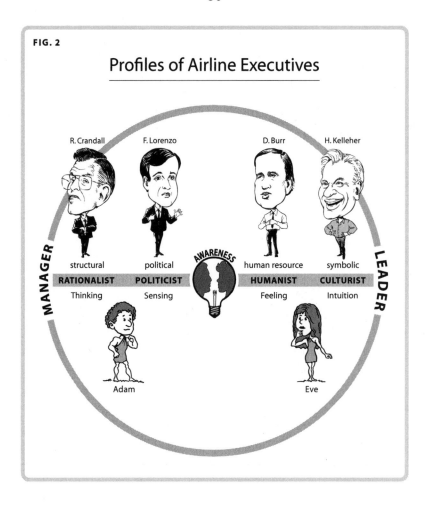

FIG. 2

## Profiles of Airline Executives

problems. Famous for its fast turnaround time, Southwest confronts security delays at congested airports. As competitors cut costs to survive, Southwest's low-fare structure will come under attack.

The U.S. airline sector demands both sound management and inspired leadership. Like most industries, it rarely gets both. The executives pictured in Figure 2 are Robert Crandall, former CEO of American Airlines; Frank Lorenzo, former CEO of Eastern Airlines; Donald Burr, former CEO of People's Express; and Herb Kelleher, former CEO of Southwest Airlines.

When we chose the airlines as a major focus, neither we nor their CEOs foresaw their planes being used as flying missiles.

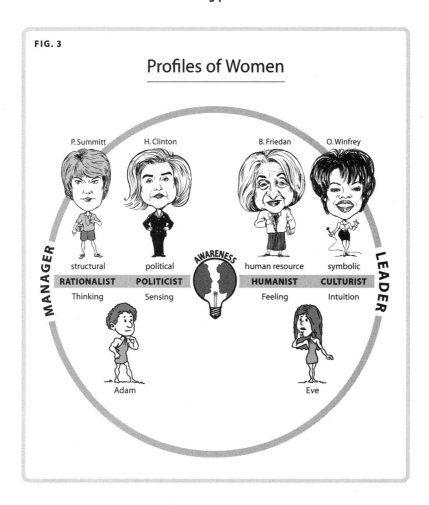

**FIG. 3**

# Profiles of Women

September 11, 2001, thrust the airlines into a new world. If they are to survive, the management and leadership skills of their executives will need to be carefully honed. An airline's two biggest assets, planes and people, demand a balanced approach: a need to make a profit while ensuring the safety of a flying public and responding to the needs of employees.

## Women in Leadership Positions

We balance the four airline executives with the four well-known women shown in Figure 3. These include Pat Summitt, head women's basketball coach at the University of Tennessee; Hillary Clinton, U.S. senator from New York; Betty Friedan, author and a founder of the women's movement; and Oprah Winfrey, television talk-show host.

More than gender equity influenced our decision regarding women. We believe, and statistics support our belief, that more women than men will eventually occupy CEO offices. This will happen not only in corporate America but in all our institutions. In addition, we believe women tend to favor the leadership side of the continuum in their roles as humanists and culturists. Could the glass ceiling actually be a "glass floor"? Women seem to better incorporate the masculine aspects of management than men do the feminine aspects of leadership.

Our reasons for selecting Summitt, Clinton, Friedan, and Winfrey are reflected in the diverse areas of society they represent. Pat Summitt continues to be a pioneer in the world of women's athletics, particularly basketball. To a great degree, she is responsible for making Title IX (the legislation enacted to level the playing field for women in intercollegiate athletics) a reality. Hillary Clinton was a formidable figure as First Lady and is becoming a powerful force in the U.S. Senate. Betty Friedan often stood alone in her struggle to free women from the "feminine mystique," a term she coined to reflect the psychic prison in which women were often trapped. The movement she helped found is a tribute to her tireless pioneering efforts. And Oprah Winfrey is a walking conglomerate in the world of television. Not only is she one of the most popular women in the world, but she is also one of the wealthiest.

## Presidents Reflect Politics

We conclude with profiles of the four U.S. presidents shown in Figure 4: Richard Nixon, the thirty-seventh president of the United States; Lyndon Johnson, the thirty-sixth president; Jimmy Carter, the thirty-ninth president; and Ronald Reagan, the fortieth U.S. president.

Few would disagree that American presidents have one of the toughest jobs in the world. At home and abroad, they must deal

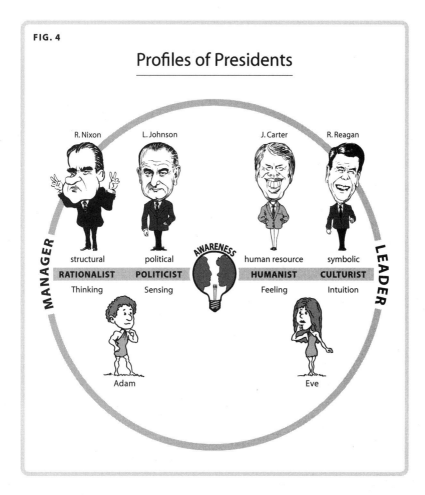

FIG. 4

## Profiles of Presidents

with special interest groups, with diverse populations, and with is-sues so complex that even a Solomon would struggle with the solu-tions. World conditions during their terms brought out the best and the worst of these four presidents. We believe they represent the range of the management-leadership spectrum as well as any presi-dents in recent history.

Each example, be it an airline CEO, an outstanding woman, or a president, should help you identify your cognitive and behavioral strengths as well as your weaknesses. A new millennium is just under way. It's a great time for both a personal and a collective be-ginning, one that we believe should balance managing and leading in a harmonious dance.

# Examining Management-Leadership Profiles

*Becoming aware of the portraits of others
and our estimates of their positions in the model
helps you discover your own position.*

# CHAPTER 3

# The Rationalist

**structural**

## Rationalist

**Thinking**

In many organizations, rationalists dominate. Rationalists prefer clarity and control to ambiguity and spontaneity. Rules, regulations, and policies guide their thinking. They focus on details and leave little to chance. In pursuit of concrete data and hard facts, rationalists often come across as cold and impersonal, interested only in objective, quantifiable things. In contrast to humanists, who make decisions based on human needs, rationalists emphasize standard operating procedures and profitability.

Organizationally, rationalists expect results and hold people accountable for their on-the-job performance. They champion efficiency and shape working conditions to produce more for less. To satisfy an obsession with the bottom line, they rely heavily on strategic planning, measurable goals, and centralized control. They see people as a means to an end, following rules and regulations set forth in policy manuals. On athletic teams, rationalists play rigidly prescribed roles dictated by manager-coaches whose playbooks mirror corporate policy manuals.

Personally, we believe, rationalists are dominated by their male archetype. They are more comfortable with reason than with emotion, with work than with pleasure. They tend to be more product oriented than people oriented. To a rationalist, people become spokes in the wheels of production. In contrast to humanists, who tend to praise and empower people, rationalists tend to supervise closely and criticize regularly. Their motive is to move people to higher levels of performance. Their impersonal style places rationalists on the left side of the management-leadership continuum, opposite humanists and culturists (see Figure 1, on page 21).

What do rationally oriented individuals look like in real life? Profiles of three highly successful, and at times controversial, managers follow. They include American Airlines former CEO Robert Crandall, University of Tennessee women's basketball coach Pat Summitt, and former president Richard Nixon. While rationality permeates their styles, none of the three is totally one-dimensional. But they appear more comfortable in the role of rationalist than in the role of politicist, humanist, or culturist.

# ROBERT CRANDALL:
# A RATIONALIST IN BUSINESS

*"The airline business is fast-paced, high-risk, and highly leveraged. It puts a premium on things I like to do.... I am very good at detail. I love detail."*

(Petzinger 1995, p. 56)

Robert Crandall's reign at American Airlines was punctuated by a push to get the company to embrace technology in every phase of its operations. In many respects, he reshaped the predominant image of American as an airline into that of a computer company. Crandall personifies the prototypical manager who is great at gathering facts and analyzing them but less adept at the intangible human side of work (see Figure 5).

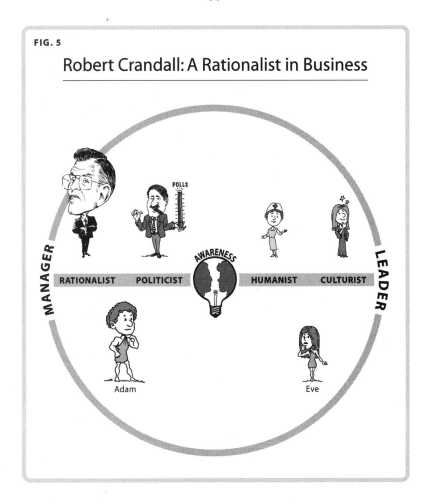

**FIG. 5**

## Robert Crandall: A Rationalist in Business

## Beginning a Facts-and-Analysis Career

Robert Crandall's penchant for facts and analysis began to emerge during his early career at Hallmark. There he championed using computers for tasks other than collecting financial data. Under his guidance, the card company developed a computer-linked inventory system that constantly monitored sales at its far-flung retail outlets. By tracking sales countrywide, Hallmark's marketing group could determine quickly which cards were outselling others. This enabled them to adjust prices and inventories in response to demand. They could pinpoint why a particular greeting card sold faster in Raleigh,

North Carolina, for example, than in other parts of the country. Such real-time information allowed Hallmark to increase prices in Raleigh while lowering them in areas where sales were slower (Petzinger 1995). Crandall's experience with Hallmark's computer system would later help him breathe new life into American Airlines' fledgling reservations system.

## The Rationalist at American Airlines

Crandall was tapped as American's CEO over competitors because of his rational approach. As Al Casey, his predecessor, pointed out, "The factor that tilted my decision toward Bob was Bob's understanding of the concept of marketing. . . . Bob understood my style, which was to establish standards and programs—everything's done by a program—with incentives, leaving nothing to chance, with good solid communications [with the troops]. Bob's a master at that" (in Reed 1993, p. 116).

A key factor in Crandall's hire was his understanding of sophisticated computer systems as marketing tools. SABRE, American's new sophisticated reservations system, evolved under his management. The function of SABRE is to balance the free-market forces of supply and demand; that is, available seats on an airplane are matched with customer purchases. Basic airline economics treats an airplane's empty seats as wasting assets. Once the airplane's payload (seats occupied by paying customers) covers labor, fuel costs, and debt service on the aircraft, every additional occupied seat represents profit. Conversely, an empty seat is an airline executive's worst nightmare.

SABRE became so critical to American's success that one writer observed,

> Under Crandall, American Airlines became the most sophisticated, the most analytical, the most heavily computerized carrier in the business. Crandall wanted quantification of everything. If an airplane was one minute late departing from the gate, if the number of no-shows exceeded what

was planned, if fewer passengers flew to a given location than expected, Crandall had to know why, and he wanted it in numbers: spread sheets, percentages, data. Crandall was the first person in the airline industry to recognize that computers could be used to process information—to analyze results, lower costs, improve sales, and ultimately increase profits. (Rubin 1993, p. 114)

Robert Crandall's attention to detail, accentuated following deregulation, soon became a driving obsession that bordered on "managerial overkill" (Reed 1993, p. 88). Two examples illustrate. First, Crandall eliminated two food items served on American flights: the olives in salads and the celery in Bloody Marys. This reduced the airline's costs by some $92,000 (Solomon 1993, p. 297); the amount varies by source). Second, Crandall suggested to a terminal manager that he reduce the number of security guards at an American warehouse. The manager complied by reducing the number from three full-time guards to one. Crandall squeezed even tighter, suggesting the remaining guard be replaced by a dog. Again, the manager complied. But Crandall did not relent: "Put a tape recorder in front of the dog and let him growl into it," he suggested (Serling 1985, p. 457). As Crandall himself acknowledges, "I am very good at detail. I love detail" (Petzinger 1995, p. 56). His wife is no stranger to his obsession. Crandall acknowledges driving her crazy by emptying and rearranging her pocketbook.

Using the statistical capabilities of SABRE, Crandall created a perpetual inventory system that allowed American to compete against People Express and other discount airlines. New low-cost airlines were posing major problems for American. They were capturing revenues at an alarming rate, primarily because their costs, particularly labor, were much lower than those of major carriers. Crandall had to come up with a way to increase revenues by attracting cost-conscious customers. Trading on his experience with real-time inventories at Hallmark, Crandall juggled seats on flights according to demand. If higher-priced tickets were not selling, American could adjust inventories, offering more seats at lower fares (Reed 1993). On any particular American flight, eight passengers might be holding tickets priced at eight different levels (Labich 1990).

## When Logic Didn't Win

Like all rationalists, Crandall had his blind spots. His rational, logical style worked to his disadvantage in American's bid to secure a prestigious route from Chicago to Tokyo. The Japan route was important to American for two reasons: Crandall desperately wanted to penetrate United's and Northwest's dominance of the Pacific Basin. In addition, he wanted to increase American's presence at Chicago's O'Hare airport, United's home turf. Reaching both objectives would contribute to Crandall's plan to achieve parity with United (Reed 1993).

The Department of Transportation (DOT) had negotiated six new routes with the Japanese government, each originating from a different U.S. city. American went after all six. United wanted only one, the Chicago-Tokyo route. As the battle heated up, politics began to dominate the issues. Immediately, Crandall was at a disadvantage. His logical mind led him to conclude that if he presented the facts in proper context, anyone with average intelligence would be persuaded. This approach might work in lengthy, detail-oriented staff meetings, but logical thinkers do not constitute a majority of either party in Washington. To the politicians, Crandall more often than not came across as abrupt, arrogant, and short-tempered (Plaskett 1996). As one writer opined, "He goes to Washington with no backing but his logic and then doesn't understand why the politicians don't see his point of view" (Reed 1996).

United, on the other hand, marshaled its political forces, conscripting stalwarts such as Chicago's powerful mayor Richard Daley and Congressman Dan Rostenkowski. Joining them was Transportation Secretary Samuel Skinner, who headed Bush's campaign in Illinois. American countered with its Washington lobbyist, William Burhop. As a result, the airline placed itself in a defensive posture. "Burhop quickly became known around the DOT and around congressional offices as 'Little Bob Crandall' because he was perceived . . . to be mimicking the angry-man approach for which his boss was so famous" (Reed 1993, p. 258).

Eventually, DOT awarded the Chicago-Tokyo route to United. Two reasons explain American's defeat: Asking for six routes only confirmed the arrogant image DOT officials held of the airline. And, probably presuming that politics was at best a dirty game, Crandall would not play outside his rationalist comfort zone.

**A Union Confrontation**

This same tendency showed itself in Crandall's understanding of the political clout of the flight attendants' union in a 1991 face-off. Denise Hedges, a longtime American flight attendant, was the union representative for the Association of Professional Flight Attendants (APFA). Under her leadership, the flight attendants represented a force that was well beyond what Crandall had surmised. He had never faced an opponent like Hedges.

In the early 1990s, Crandall was forced to attack American's costs directly, and labor received the frontal assault. Because he thought flight attendants could be easily replaced, Crandall targeted them for a pay cut. However, once he threw down the gauntlet, Hedges picked it up, backed by the solid support of her peers. As one writer observed, it was Delilah taking on Samson, and Crandall would get a haircut he would never forget (Ott and Neidl 1995).

Hedges coached the flight attendants for the coming battle with meticulous precision. Aided by labor consultants, the flight attendants received a crash course on how to survive a strike. Hedges calculated the company would have replacements ready in eleven days and took note that Thanksgiving was just around the corner. Hedges knew that Thanksgiving is an airline's busiest time of the year. A strike during that time would accomplish two things: It would get the attention of management and garner the support of holiday travelers (Petzinger 1995). Just before the holiday, the attendants walked out. As they picketed in front of the nation's airports, they chanted, "They lied to you. Now you know what we go through" (p. 415).

As a result of American's tight schedules and federal regulations requiring every flight to be serviced by a certain number of attendants, the strike shut down 20 percent of American's flights and affected another 40 percent in one way or another. Estimates at the time put American's losses at $10 million a day (Ott and Neidl 1995). After four days, President Clinton stepped in and convinced both sides to submit to arbitration. Some believe that had the strike continued another six days, American would have gone under. A national magazine quoted Crandall's dire forecast: "Unless the world changes, we will never buy another plane. We won't replace the airplanes that wear out. . . . The company simply won't be here anymore" (in Petzinger 1995, p. 415).

Crandall mistakenly assumed that he could weather a flight attendant's strike and that the attendants could be replaced with little or no interruption to operations. He failed to consider the far-reaching effects of American's high-volume hub-and-spoke system in which the slightest glitch would throw the airline's domestic schedule into disarray. Nor did he consider public opinion. If women were perceived as being exploited, what would be the backlash? Crandall had gotten himself into a fight he could not handle and, like a bully calling on his big brother for help, he called on the president, a tactic he would resort to again when pushed into a corner by his pilots (Bryant 1997).

## Crandall's Legacy: A Computerized Bureaucracy

Crandall's penchant for control also became evident in the airline's "Committing to Leadership Program." This program was aimed at giving employees more discretion and a greater sense of ownership in the company. As it evolved, American's management became concerned that control over areas such as safety, scheduling, and maintenance was being eroded by the empowerment ideals of Committing to Leadership. An American official described this paradox as one end pushing on the other: "In the middle was considerable inertia from decades of the old management style" (Loveman 1992, p. 6). In a training video for employees, Crandall analyzed the clash between the old and the new, which he described as "the need for flexibility demanded by Committing to Leadership and the pervasive need for operational rigidity in the airline business" (p. 7).

Crandall believes he knows more about every aspect of a problem confronting American than do those directly involved in its solution. He is often perceived as a micromanager, so focused on the trees that he forgets the forest. A former associate observed,

> Bob's intensity is focused on problems. He is very analytical and attacks a problem like a bulldog. His approach to solving a problem is often taken personally by those around him. [However] this is his intensity toward the problem, not toward people. He wants to be involved in every detail; he wants to be the one to determine if it's done right. (Plaskett 1996)

In an interview conducted after his retirement from American, Crandall seemed to concur. To the statement, "A lot of your innovations . . . seem to be attempts to control, constrain potentially ruinous competition," Crandall responded that the innovations were his response to changing conditions in the industry (Solomon 1998). To the question, "Looking back, would you soften your style at all?" Crandall answered, "All that toughness was more a function of media representation than of reality." When pressed further, he said, "I'm tough enough to do what has to be done when it must be done."

## Dancing with His Opposite

We see Crandall's attempts to disregard the flight attendants as his internal struggles to embrace his opposite. Note our estimate of the size of his Eve (the humanist and the culturist) in relation to his Adam (the rationalist and the politicist). The area of human resources was almost always the first to come under scrutiny when costs rose at American. When flight attendants challenged Crandall's policies, he might have thought he could suppress them as easily as he had suppressed his Eve.

By embracing more of his humanist and culturist facets, would Crandall have been more successful? A videotape he made honoring rival Herb Kelleher reveals a softer side. Aired at a recognition dinner, the video features Crandall dressed in a tuxedo, singing "He Did It His Way," accompanying himself on the piano. Crandall's creative and human tribute acknowledged Kelleher's leading Southwest to another industry milestone.

## PAT SUMMITT: A RATIONALIST IN WOMEN'S ATHLETICS

*"When you sit in the big chair, you must make tough, unpopular decisions.... As a manager, you are responsible."*
(Summitt with Jenkins 1998, p. 31)

Glass ceilings have never been an impediment to Pat Summitt, women's basketball coach at the University of Tennessee. She says, "You can scream and kick at [them] and try to shatter [them] with your high heels. Or you can learn to cut glass. I chose to be a glass cutter" (Summitt with Jenkins 1998, p. 154). The glass-cutting Summitt has led the "Lady Vols" of Tennessee to fourteen Final Four appearances and six NCAA championships, numbers that undoubtedly will increase before she retires. Together with archrival Geno Auriemma, women's coach at Connecticut, Summitt reigns atop the U.S. women's collegiate basketball world. Summitt has been named national coach of the year four times, and she is the all-time "winningest" coach in women's basketball history. In international competition, her record is sixty-three and four. She has coached numerous All-Americans and three players named National Player of the Year. Eleven former team members have played on U.S. Olympic teams. In October 2000, Summitt was inducted into the Naismith Basketball Hall of Fame. Perhaps the ultimate compliment was paid Summitt by C. M. Newton, director of athletics at Kentucky. When Newton hired Rick Pitino to head aguably the most celebrated men's basketball program in the country, he confessed that Summitt had been in the running for the job (Smith 2000a).

Summitt often speaks of herself as being two people: Trish Head, the shy, tomboyish farm girl who grew up in tiny Henrietta, Tennessee, and Pat Summitt, the tall, slender fashion model who walks the sidelines of basketball courts across the country (Summitt with Jenkins 1998, pp. 24, 25). Reconciling these two personalities is a work in progress, one that Summitt approaches with the same zeal with which she pursues national championships.

Summitt describes herself as a type-A personality. "What that means," she says, "is I'm authoritative. I'm one of those people who feels like I have an invisible hand in the small of my back, pushing me. I have a sense of urgency about everything, even doing laundry" (Summitt with Jenkins 1998, p. 143). Figure 6 depicts our assessment of her profile.

During their careers at Tennessee, the young women who play for Summitt experience every aspect of her "authoritarian" style. Her hand is constantly in the smalls of their backs, pushing them to their limits, and every time they get knocked down, she demands they get up. Summitt is an imposing presence on the basketball court. Dressed immaculately, the tall, svelte coach stalks the side-lines with a glare that conveys one message: Do it my way or you'll be over here on the bench. In Summitt's mind, her players should get every rebound, gather up every loose ball, and make every shot. Game officials are held to similar exacting standards.

Summitt's attempt to control every aspect of her team's play does not end on the floor. During halftimes, Lady Vol players sit in desk chairs as though in a classroom while Summitt lectures at a board in the front of the locker room. Her admonitions concern breakdowns in the offensive and defensive systems she expects her players to execute to perfection. Like a CEO conducting perfor-mance reviews with managers, she gives feedback on mistakes made during the first twenty minutes of play and then proceeds to outline what she expects from each player during the second half. Nothing is left to chance.

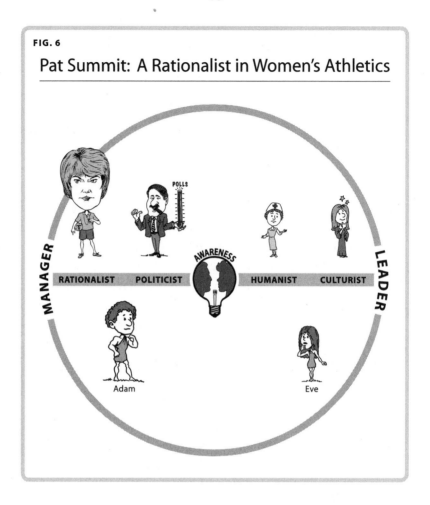

**FIG. 6**

## Pat Summit: A Rationalist in Women's Athletics

MANAGER · RATIONALIST · POLITICIST · AWARENESS · HUMANIST · CULTURIST · LEADER

Adam  Eve

## Pat Knows

So powerful is Summitt's control that her players believe she knows things about them before they actually happen—or at least soon thereafter. Summitt thrives on the omniscient image she has created in their minds. As she says,

> I tend to perpetuate the idea that "Pat Knows," because it's an effective way of imposing order . . . and demanding high standards. . . . While I don't want my players or my son to be afraid of me, I do want them to have a healthy respect for the consequences if they cross me. . . . Our Tennessee

players have to think that just about anything is better than facing me. (Summitt with Jenkins 1998, pp. 92–93)

Summitt's players are not the only ones who respect her authoritative approach. A Tennessee motorist also found out how tough she can be. Pregnant with son Tyler, Summitt, along with one of her assistants, became ensnarled in a long line of traffic on the way home from the Knoxville airport. An overweight, tattooed motorist, using the median as a passing lane, attempted to pass Summitt. She cut in front of the man's car, forcing him to pull in behind her. When he gave her the finger and cursed her, Summitt got out of her car and challenged the motorist. Poking him in the chest, she told him, "If you ever do that to me again, I'll whip your butt" (pp. 45–46).

"Whipping butts" came naturally to Summitt. She describes the early childhood environment that fostered it. "Nobody in the family seemed to regard me as a girl when it came to work or playing basketball," she says. "I fought hard and played hard, and I was expected to hold my own with my brothers, whether we were in the fields or in the hayloft" (where her father had built a basketball court). Summitt was forty-three when she received her first hug from her father (pp. 20–21).

## A Cinderella Season

Broken spirits seemed the order of the day in Tennessee's 1997 "Cinderella season." The team was plagued by injuries, more defeats (ten) than any championship team in history, and a passive attitude that Summitt would not let them forget. In the end, the Lady Vols rode an emotional roller-coaster from "tears to triumph" and ended up with a repeat national championship ("Cinderella Season" 1998). It was perhaps Summitt's finest hour as she had to adapt to innumerable changes. Yet, like every successful leader, Summitt knows that "the willingness to . . . change may be the most essential ingredient to success" (Summitt with Jenkins 1998, p. 221). That she can change is obvious. Every year she recruits new players, faces new game situations, and reaches new heights. To Summitt, new heights are measured by national championships.

She applies her controlling tactics not only to her players, but also to herself. After Duke upset Tennessee in the national tournament, Summitt began wearing a Duke shirt when jogging, a reminder that losing is not fun.

# A Storied Coach

Two stories reveal Summitt's demanding style and her attempts to remain flexible. One involves the recruitment of star player Michelle Marciniak, the other a visit with Phil Jackson, former coach of the Chicago Bulls.

### Recruiting Marciniak

Summit was pregnant when she and assistant Mickie DeMoss flew to Pennsylvania to sell Michelle Marciniak on attending the University of Tennessee. At Marciniak's home, Summitt went into labor, but she refused to leave until she had met with the young recruit. After the visit, she and DeMoss rushed to the airport and boarded a private plane to return to Knoxville. While in flight, the pilots radioed ahead to Roanoke, Virginia. There they planned to land and rush Summitt to the hospital. Summitt, however, had a problem with that plan. The University of Virginia had beaten the Lady Vols that year, keeping them from reaching the Final Four. Summit refused to land in Virginia and told the pilots to continue to Knoxville. The pilots obeyed, and Summit gave birth to her son in a Tennessee hospital, but Marciniak decided to attend Notre Dame (Summitt with Jenkins 1998).

The Marciniak saga does not end there, however. Eventually she transferred from Notre Dame to play for the Lady Vols. Her relationship with Summitt fluctuated between love and hate. Following a tough loss, Summitt afforded no mercy in her verbal abuse of Marciniak, then a senior. Having wrestled with her emotions throughout the night, Marciniak called Summitt early the next morning to vent her displeasure: "I don't need to be ridden all the time and just lashed out at, like you've been doing in front of my teammates. I'm not responding to that" ("Have Mercy" 2000, p. 56). To Summitt's credit, she reflected on Marciniak's words and realized she had been wrong: "Sometimes I'm more stubborn than I am smart. But that time, I decided I needed to be smart about this. I needed to give in. Michelle was about to break, and the one thing you never want to do is break a player's spirit" (p. 56). It was one of the rare times Summitt allowed her dance partner to lead.

After her playing career, Marciniak reflected, "Off the court, she's really a person who cares about people and what happens to her players" (Smith 2000a, p. D1). Similar sentiments were echoed by Summitt's college sorority sister Mary Carter, after her son was killed in an accident. "After Caleb was killed, she was so supportive. She's strong and she's tough . . . but people didn't see the other side of her. They didn't see the tears from a mother's standpoint" (p. D1).

### Visiting Jackson

It's no secret that Connecticut is a thorn in the side of Pat Summitt. Year in and year out, it seems that either the Lady Huskies or the Lady Vols are ranked number one in the national polls. In 1996, Summit was watching films of a game between Tennessee and Connecticut. As she studied Connecticut's offense, Summitt realized that it was causing her team a number of problems, and, worse, she didn't understand why. Not one to take losing lightly, Summitt decided to do something about her frustration. She and her staff flew to Chicago to learn the intricacies of the system. With Phil Jackson in the film room, Summitt viewed film after film of the Bulls in action. What she observed was a system that allowed great players (particularly Jordan of the Bulls) to use their talents within certain team principles. Reflecting on the trip, Summitt said, "He [Jackson] lets people be who they want to be within his framework. For me, that's an area where I've had to change. Since that trip, I'm more tolerant than ever before" (Summitt with Jenkins 1998, pp. 226–227). If Jackson could allow another dimension on the court, so could she in providing an example of a waltz with the opposite part of herself.

Summitt honed her skills back in Henrietta, the small rural Tennessee community in which she grew up. Making the United States Women's Basketball Team was but the first step toward realizing a vision that embraced making a "difference for [all] women." Summitt explains,

> Sports, it struck me, could be a vital avenue to self-worth for women. It was for me. That shows you what a game can do: It can teach you to explore and broaden your capabilities. That's why the explosion in female athletic participation over the last twenty years has been so important. Think about it. There was actually a time when women were forbidden to run marathons for fear we'd damage our ovaries. Basketball for women was stationary, to make sure we didn't swoon. But unfettered play affords the experience of excellence, both physically and mentally. It is too critical for personal development to deny it to half the population. (p. 23)

Without question, Summitt continues to be a powerful force in assuring that basketball is not denied to "half the population." The rapid growth of women's participation in the sport is largely a result of her untiring efforts. Through her iron-fisted, hands-on approach, Summitt has created an image of legendary proportions, not only in the minds of her opponents, but in the minds of her players as well.

## Dancing with Her Opposite

After observing Phil Jackson's style, Summitt realized that she had to become more tolerant of her players' features and foibles. In basketball a rigid style can squelch creativity, especially when a coach is blessed with great players. Chamique Holdsclaw, Tennessee's National Player of the Year in 1998 and 1999, was Summitt's Michael Jordan. To capitalize on Holdsclaw's extraordinary talents, Summitt needed to give her more freedom within the Tennessee offense. Summitt gave it and, in doing so, seemed to recognize that her structured way of doing things needed more flexibility.

Summitt's growing awareness of the need to dance with her opposite shows she is able to step back and observe her weaknesses. "I hire people who have qualities I'm deficient in," she acknowledges. "By evaluating my own strengths and weaknesses, I can put people in position to complement me. It means setting aside your ego. But it's a far more sensible way of doing business than to insist on being right all the time" (Summitt with Jenkins 1998, p. 150).

Summitt is also aware of her Lady Vols' chief nemesis: Connecticut's Lady Huskies. When they played before twenty-four thousand fans at Tennessee, it was the largest crowd in the history of the women's game. At the time, Connecticut was ranked number one and Tennessee was ranked number two. It was the sixth meeting between the schools while occupying the top two spots in the polls. Connecticut has won five of those six contests and claims an eleven-to-six advantage overall.

How has Geno Auriemma, whose Lady Huskies have won four NCAA championships and recently set a women's record of seventy consecutive wins, made such inroads onto the turf long dominated by Pat Summitt, the first women's coach to reach eight hundred wins? When asked about his success, Auriemma pointed to a picture of his players that appeared in *Sports Illustrated*. The photo showed his players on the sideline cheering for their teammates on the floor. Auriemma said, "That picture says it all . . . we bring emotion to basketball" (Rosenfield 1997). The following statement on a picture in Auriemma's office seems to sum up his style: "Passion. There are many things in life that will catch your eye, but only a few will catch your heart. Pursue those" (Rosenfield 1997). He represents passion, Summitt precision.

# RICHARD NIXON:
# A RATIONALIST IN THE PRESIDENCY

*"[S]he [Nixon's mother, Hannah] never indulged in the present-day custom, which I find nauseating, of hugging and kissing her children.... I can never remember her saying 'I love you'—she didn't have to."*

*(Aitken 1993, pp. 14–15)*

At first glance, Richard Nixon appears a consummate politician with an occasional flare for drama. But, beneath the surface, Nixon was a rationalist—in control, concerned about minute details, and

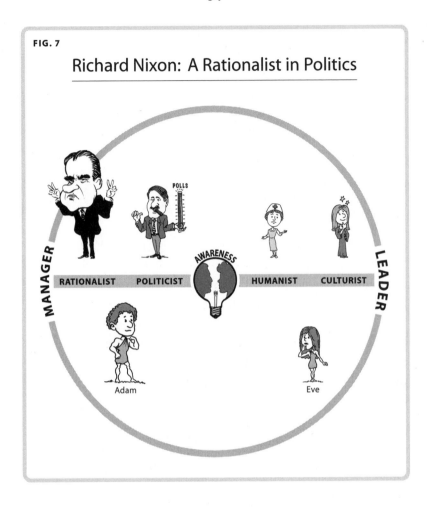

FIG. 7

Richard Nixon: A Rationalist in Politics

emotionally distant. Notice our estimate of Nixon's management-leadership profile in Figure 7.

Nixon's rational leanings began to develop in early boyhood. His father helped him win a debate in which boys were underdogs to the girls. The subject was "Resolved: That insects are more harmful than beneficial." Demonstrating his determination to win through paying attention to details, Nixon had his father drive him to Riverside. There he sought the expert advice of an uncle, who "pointed out that without bees and other insects that carry pollen from tree to tree and bush to bush, all foliage would die" (Nixon 1990, p. 87).

Nixon's interest in debating continued throughout his political life. As a debater, he had few equals. His style reflected "intensive preparation, [mean-spirited] rhetoric, and single-handed decision-making" (Barber 1992, p. 141). It was his linear thinking that cost Nixon the 1960 presidential debate with John F. Kennedy. Nixon assumed that winning a debate was more about fact and logic than appearance and style. Explaining his loss, Nixon believed he had mastered the "substance" of the debate. Even so, he confessed, "I looked tired, and I had foolishly not put on makeup to compensate for the bags under my eyes and my five-o'clock shadow" (Nixon 1990, p. 137). Before the debate, he refused his aides' advice to wear makeup, choosing to follow his own counsel, a trait that continually haunted him later on.

Nixon's rigidity and struggle to maintain control kept him remote and aloof. When Nixon was entertaining the highly esteemed Kennedy pollster Lou Harris in the Oval Office, he asked Harris, "Do you think I can be a personality kid?" After explaining what he meant, Nixon continued, "My staff thinks I can. I think I've got a lousy personality, and I'm not a personality kid." When Harris responded, "Mr. President, people don't like your personality," Nixon seemed relieved (Matthews 1996, p. 282).

One reporter candidly observed Nixon's penchant for being in control. "You didn't have to be around him very long [before] realizing that he was a . . . highly programmed man. I had the impression he would even practice his inflection when he said, 'Hello'" (Matthews 1996, p. 59).

Another incident supports this observation. While walking on a California beach, Nixon attempted to emulate the charismatic image John Kennedy projected. But Nixon was unable to pull it off. He wore his regular street clothes—slacks and wing-tipped shoes, with a windbreaker—and he stuck out like the proverbial sore thumb (Gannon 1994).

## An Iron-Fisted White House

Observing former presidents Ford, Carter, and Nixon aligned along a dais at a Washington social event, former senator Bob Dole quipped, "See no evil [Ford], hear no evil [Carter], and evil [Nixon]!" (Gergen 2000, p. 19). Dole was not alone in his appraisal of the presidents. Many Americans came to believe that Nixon personified evil and that his White House was awash in it.

In his book *Eyewitness to Power,* former White House speechwriter David Gergen argues that Nixon continually confused "the exercise of power" with "the exercise of leadership" (2000, p. 46). According to Gergen, Nixon believed that only great men could rule authoritatively; hence, his rationalization for mistrusting basic democratic processes.

Nixon ran the White House with an iron fist, always in control. Gergen describes the process:

> When Haldeman's office called, you jumped. Action was demanded now, no questions asked. Even—as it was for Dwight [Chapin, a young aide]—if it was illegal . . . like so much else in the Nixon operation, the zeal to win, to control every detail, to make the trains run on time, went completely overboard. It wasn't just efficient—which would have been fine—but was turned into a Marine boot camp. The system worked from the top down and brooked no dissent from the bottom up. (pp. 94, 96)

To Gergen, "one of Nixon's worst sins was to create a reign of intimidation and a culture of expectation that his finest young men should march over a cliff for him" (pp. 96–97). Nixon had, in effect, "established a government within a government—a rogue operation at the White House" (p. 100).

Alluding to Nixon's internal demons, Gergen says, "There were fires burning within him that were not well suited to the demands of leadership in our democratic system" (p. 65). Nixon simply could not trust people. Rather than empowering people Nixon sought to control them, a trait of the typical manager. Because Nixon's feeling side had been sealed off, Gergen "saw . . . a man who did not relate well to others and who seemed to deny softer, emotional feelings, choosing instead to face the world with a harsh steeliness" (p. 80).

Nixon's tendency to suppress his feelings surfaced early. In high school he enjoyed performing in plays. But even in fictional roles Nixon's rational side overruled his emotional side. In Virgil's *Aeneid*, he played Aeneas, and his girlfriend (Ola-Florence Welch) played Dido. "At one point, a very dramatic moment," he recalls, "the script calls for Aeneas and Dido to embrace; in fact, it calls for Aeneas to kiss Dido. I wouldn't do that, but at least we agreed that we would embrace" (Gannon 1994). Later, during Nixon's presidency, a military aide jokingly described one of his duties as "briefing Nixon on how to kiss his wife" (Abrahamsen 1977, p. 241).

## Nixon's Fourth Branch of Government

A penchant for control motivated Nixon to build the structural walls of the executive branch higher and higher. To him, the founding fathers did not get it right with the system of checks and balances they built into our three branches of government. He felt compelled to establish a "fourth branch." Jonathan Schell explains Nixon's preoccupation with reorganizing the White House:

> Since arriving in office, President Nixon had developed the conviction that a powerful "Establishment" consisting of the senate, the antiwar movement, the press, the television networks, and independent foundations was plotting to cripple the American presidency and to destroy him personally at the earliest possible date, and now he had arrived at the conclusion that the federal bureaucracy, too, was in on the plot. (1975, p. 106)

By bringing additional agencies under the aegis of a "fourth branch," Nixon had "set up his own little government on top of the Constitutional one" (Barber 1992, p. 145) and, in so doing, set in motion a battle plan Nixon speechwriter Pat Buchanan described as "striking at the heart of the Establishment" (Schell 1975, p. 85). Thus, in effect, Nixon had established a tyrannical operation out of the White House, one that:

made secret war . . . made secret agreements to sell immense quantities of deadly weapons to nervous nations . . . supported foreign governments which ruled by terror . . . received bribes and sold high offices . . . recruited and operated a secret White House police force and ordered them to break the law, continually and casually . . . abrogated Congress's power . . . subverted important segments of the electoral system, the judicial system, the law enforcement system, the tax system, and the free speech system. (Barber 1992, p. 144)

To Nixon these efforts were legitimate presidential exercises of authority. Reaching important goals required an authority structure that would leave nothing to chance.

## Managerial Style

During the Watergate hearings, White House aide Alexander Butterfield described Nixon's micromanagement of social functions.

The President often, of course, was concerned whether or not the curtains were closed or open; the arrangements of state gifts; whether they should be on that side of the room or this side of the room; displayed on a weekly basis or on a monthly basis. . . . He was deeply involved in the entertainment business—whom we should get, for what kind of group, small band, big band, black band, white band, jazz band, whatever. He was very interested in meals and how they were served and the time of the waiters. . . . He wanted to see the plan, see the scenarios; he wanted to view the musical selections himself. He was very interested in whether or not salad should be served and decided that at small dinners of eight or less the salad course should not be served. . . . [He] took a detailed interest in the pageantry of White House occasions. . . . [He] wanted to know whether or not [it] should be public on the south grounds or whether we should have administrative personnel; the details of the walk up the driveway; whether the military should be to the right or left; which uniforms would be worn by the White House police; whether or not the Secret Service would salute during "The Star Spangled Banner" and sing; where the photographer would be. (in Schell 1975, p. 285)

When key episodes in Nixon's life—the "Checkers Speech," the Alger Hiss case, the bombing of Cambodia, and ultimately Watergate—are joined, they portray a life history that conjures up images of an archipelago, a chain of islands linked by one continuous bridge: a rigid style of self-management. Nixon began constructing his "bridge" in boyhood. He nurtured it in young adulthood and added the finishing links during his presidency. The overriding function of his style was designed to aid him in navigating what he perceived to be the treacherous waters of the Establishment. Supporting Nixon's personal edifice were a number of complex structural girders: an obsessive attention to detail; rhetorical skills that left less logical opponents cut to shreds; role-playing adjusted to fit a particular scenario; an obsessive need to control, demonstrated in his constant reorganization of the executive branch and his own persona; and repressed memories of early struggles that drove him unmercifully toward success, which he measured as "getting back" at the Establishment.

## A "Spy" in the White House

Chris Matthews referred to the taping system Nixon installed in the Oval Office as being a "robot spy" (1999). "Robot" describes Nixon the man and Nixon the president as no other metaphor could. Some five hundred hours of tapes are now in the public domain. Together, they expose a man who trusted few and saw the worst in all. The Oval Office tapes reveal the dark side of a man who plotted against his enemies with a vengeance bordering on deep paranoia.

Nixon was a man whose feelings were apparently almost totally suppressed. The tapes reveal his need to control and his compulsion to exact revenge on those who attempted to thwart his authority. If nothing else, the tapes show us a man who was his own worst enemy. Never in his wildest dreams did Nixon imagine an electronic system that was installed to reinforce his view of history ending up as the "smoking gun" indicting him as one of history's saddest cases.

Asked to explain how Nixon became entangled in the Watergate cover-up, George Schultz, who served in Nixon's cabinet, said, "He had a tormented side along with an extraordinarily gifted and good side, and the tormented side brought him down" (Matthews 1999).

## Dancing with His Opposite

When a military aide described his job as "briefing Nixon on how to kiss his wife," he was saying what many Americans already suspected: Nixon was personally cold and distant. He typically showed little, if any, emotion. Eisenhower added to this perception of emotional distance when he said Nixon needed to work at being a nice guy instead of trying to look like one.

To dance with his opposite, Nixon had much to learn. He holds a dominant position on the continuum's management side. We attribute that to his Eve being isolated in his psyche. To Nixon, embracing his feminine side would no doubt reflect weakness. He went to great lengths to convince the public that he was in control. This meant covering up his weaknesses and showing little emotion.

Had Nixon been more comfortable with his soft side, he might have been comfortable with others. He might have learned to trust others and perhaps, in the process, honor his own feelings. His Eve might have enticed him to dance as a feeling human being, not as a robot.

## THREE PROFILES, ONE STYLE

Examine the characteristics of these three managers who favor a rational approach to running their organizations. Do you see yourself managing like Crandall, Summitt, or Nixon? Concentrate on their styles, not on their personalities.

- Are you prone to focus on details when facing a task?
- Do you find yourself wanting to get to the facts, to the bottom line, brushing aside how someone might feel about an issue?
- Do you have a tendency to be uncomfortable when not in control of a situation?

If you find yourself answering these questions in the affirmative, then, more than likely, a rationalist approach captures your dominant style. Let's review the three profiles to tease out their common learnings.

## Crandall

The portrait of Crandall shows him dominated by rationalist logic. Recall that rationalists like to create structures that foster clarity and control, leaving little to chance. They tend to be dominated by their Adam archetypes, and, as a result, their Eves are largely overlooked. Notice that our appraisal of Crandall's Adam is much larger than his Eve.

Observing Crandall's style shows much more of a rationalist than a politicist, humanist, or culturist. Although he was very effective at analyzing and solving many of American's problems, Crandall had trouble recognizing and dealing with human issues, particularly those of employees. His ongoing war with American's flight attendants is one example of Crandall's inability to dance with his opposite.

## Summitt

One sees Summitt on the far left of the continuum, dominated by her rationalist leanings, much as was Crandall. Rationalists like to be in control and tend to be influenced by their masculine archetype. We see Summitt's Adam much larger than her Eve.

When Summitt describes her job, the picture becomes clearer.

> When you sit in the big chair, you must make tough, unpopular decisions, because you are responsible for the group and the greater good. . . . If you don't have the stomach for unpleasant tasks, for firing people, fighting battles, or breaking bad news—and doing it forthrightly—you shouldn't be in that position. In a management job, every knock on your door represents a potential problem. Every single one. As a manager you are responsible. (Summitt with Jenkins 1998, p. 31)

Summitt's authoritative approach, coupled with her tendency to control, explains our depiction of her as a rationalist. Demands she places on herself know no bounds. At times, she loses sight of her own needs, as well as those of her players. In the Marciniak story, as we saw, Summitt was determined her child would be born in Tennessee. But at what price? If Summitt is this hard on herself, imagine the emotional rigors her players might endure. This tendency could very well limit Summitt's ability to dance with her opposite.

## Nixon

As with Crandall and Summit, we place Nixon on the far left of the model. Rationalists draw heavily on their authority and create structures to foster clarity and control. We also depict Nixon's Adam much larger than his Eve.

The robotlike image Nixon projected reflected a man obsessed with control. He did not seem able to let himself go. Nixon appeared not at home with his feelings or comfortable with others, even his wife. Getting in touch with his emotional side was very difficult for Nixon; hence his difficulty in relating with his Eve.

Crandall, Summit, and Nixon are very effecient individuals. They illustrate what rationalists are all about. The question is could they be (or have been) even more successful by learning to dance with their humanist and culturist opposites? If you did not recognize your personal style in these profiles, read on. Your preferred approach may lie elsewhere. As you reflect, keep in mind that all four styles—the rationalist, politicist, humanist, and culturist—are part of you, regardless of your dominant type.

# The Politicist

political
## Politicist
**Sensing**

Shrewd and astute in their determination to implement chosen agenda, politically oriented leaders are often labeled manipulative, unethical, and territorial. Their quest for power and influence earns them a bad name. But removing politics from organizations would ensure that very little would ever get done.

As they "stump" through organizations, politicists see constituents face-to-face, talk to them about problems, and listen to their opinions. They "press the flesh," shaking hands with people from all walks of life. Polls and surveys serve as compasses in navigating their territory. Polls tell politicists how they are doing and how constituencies rate their performance. Surveys reflect what constituents are sensing, what issues are affecting them, and what they expect representatives to do.

Politicists shrewdly set a course of action that will achieve desired ends. Once their power base is established, they mobilize support, neutralize their opposition, and negotiate and bargain toward a workable outcome. In contrast to culturists, who focus on the future and its possibilities, politicists focus on the realities of the present.

Many politicists guard the public's trust in an honest and forthright manner. Others do not. Still, a political orientation is a key ingredient in effective management and leadership.

How do politicists muster the clout necessary to achieve their agenda when available resources are limited? To shed light on the process, we offer profiles of three politically oriented, at times controversial, individuals: former Eastern Airlines CEO Frank Lorenzo, New York senator Hillary Clinton, and former president Lyndon Johnson. None of the three is one-dimensional, even though they all appear to be more comfortable in the role of politicist than in the role of rationalist, humanist, or culturist.

As you encounter Lorenzo, Clinton, and Johnson you may become resistant and want to tune out. Deserving or not, politics today has a bad image and many people are unwilling to play the game or admit to their political leanings. A more neutral stance, however, would acknowledge that little gets done in the absence of clear agenda, adequate political muscle, supportive coalitions, and a knack for bargaining and negotiation. In today's world, politics and leadership are inseparable, and, as Jeffrey Pfeffer explains in *Managing with Power* (1994), there is a promising path between muggers' alley and idealistic naïveté. To walk the fine line between the two is the only way to get what you want. To survive and win in any organization, you either suit up or watch the game from the sidelines. The following three examples show political players at work.

# FRANK LORENZO:
# A POLITICIST IN BUSINESS

*"[A] boss they love to hate"; possessing a mind*
*"that would make Machiavelli look like Gomer Pyle."*
(Schwartz, Calonius, Gonzalez, and Gibney 1989, p. 20)

Frank Lorenzo was often depicted as the airline industry's Darth Vader. And, whether or not he read Machiavelli's *The Prince*,

**FIG. 8**

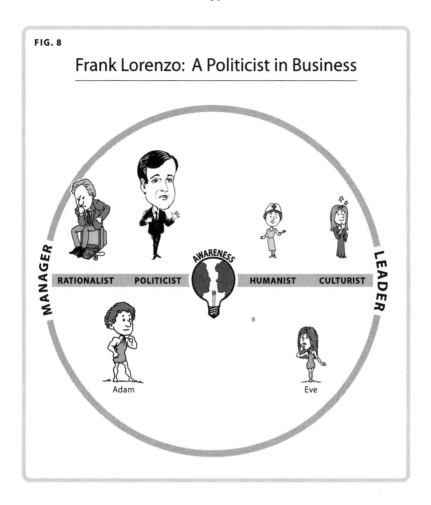

Frank Lorenzo: A Politicist in Business

Lorenzo adhered to many of the book's tenets. He relied heavily on political guile and shrewdness in building one of America's largest airline empires. Like the prince, he accumulated enemies and ruined people's lives along the way. But his skill in maneuvering and getting his way sheds some light on important political lessons for both managers and leaders. Note his profile in Figure 8.

## A Young Howard Hughes?

Two men, Lorenzo's father and Howard Hughes, were influential in creating the early script for Lorenzo's later accomplishments.

Shrewdly investing the profits from his small retail business, the senior Lorenzo accumulated a diversified portfolio of securities. As a young man, Lorenzo followed his father's lead and began purchasing shares of stock in Trans World Airlines (TWA). This early experience with the ups and downs of investing, coupled with his father's struggles in a tough retailing environment, made an indelible impression on the young financier. Lorenzo's other financial role model was Howard Hughes (Petzinger 1995). Following Hughes' example, Lorenzo early demonstrated an uncanny ability to attract investors and to manipulate financial statements. This fiscal wizardry continued throughout his career (Barrett 1987).

Lorenzo's aspirations led him to Harvard Business School, where he met Bob Carney. Following graduation and brief separate careers, the two formed a partnership in 1966. Each partner contributed a meager $1,000 to found Lorenzo, Carney, and Company. The young entrepreneurs then set out to pursue their business plan, marketing themselves as "experts in aviation finance" ready to assist companies in financial trouble (Petzinger 1995). Three years later, Lorenzo and Carney decided to incorporate to secure additional capital. In doing so, they gained control of a large pool of money in which their personal stake was less than 3 percent. Lorenzo and Carney's creation of Jet Capital displayed their uncanny Midas touch.

Jet Capital quickly moved from an initial leasing orientation to an ownership mode. Lorenzo explained the change: "It occurred to me . . . that we could offer a combination of financial advice and equity participation—after all, Jet Capital still had the proceeds of that stock sale—to companies that were in dire need of it" (Barrett 1987, p. 101). With their new business plan in place, Lorenzo and Carney began to go after struggling airlines, like lions stalking prey.

## Stalking Prey

Mohawk Airlines was their first takeover target. But, after studying Lorenzo's proposal, Mohawk's directors were less than impressed with the subtle power play camouflaged in the plan. They voted to merge with Allegheny instead (Petzinger 1995).

Turning their attention south, Lorenzo and Carney focused on financially troubled Texas International, an airline locals jokingly referred to as "Tree Top Airlines" because it struggled to get off the ground (Murphy 1986). Texas International desperately needed an infusion of capital. Lorenzo and Carney were poised with a purse, but this time their financial plans required a third-party player. Donald Burr's National Aviation met the requirements. Burr's company contributed part of the $5 million Lorenzo estimated they needed (Petzinger 1995). But more important than the immediate deal was the tumultuous relationship that later developed between Burr and Lorenzo.

## Landing in Texas

Lorenzo became CEO of Texas International and soon went head-to-head with his nemesis—organized labor. Despite some early financial success, labor costs continued to rise, as did union militancy. In December 1974, Texas International ground workers walked off their jobs. Lorenzo fought back by grounding the company's fleet from December to April. When workers returned to work, they did so under terms dictated by management. Lorenzo drew the battle line between himself and labor, the "bad guys," and quickly became "a boss they love to hate" (Schwartz et al. 1989, p. 20).

Lorenzo's next target was National Airlines. The company's debt was small compared to that of other carriers—less than $50 million—and its asssets were valued at $600 million (Cook 1978). Lorenzo was convinced that National could be acquired without Texas International having to leverage its own funds. Stealthily, Texas International began to accumulate shares in National. When news of Lorenzo's scheme leaked out, Pan American entered the bidding war. As a result, the price of National's shares soared. The politically astute Lorenzo sold his shares, pocketing $35 million (after taxes), a return of approximately 800 percent (Petzinger 1995).

Looking to expand his base of power, Lorenzo then set his sights on TWA, and in 1979 he met with TWA's chairman, Edwin Smart. However, Lorenzo's pomposity so enraged Smart that he bolted from the breakfast table. Smart refused to believe that the CEO of an airline one-tenth the size of his would try to absorb TWA (Ennis 1988).

Following the less than amicable meeting with Smart, Lorenzo created a new subsidiary, New York Air. It would offer flights to compete with Eastern's shuttle service (Engardio et al. 1986). For $49, business travelers could travel at almost any time, with fares barely above the cost of a bus ticket (Moritz 1987). But this time the union reacted to the deal by making the La Guardia–based carrier the target of a $1 million pilots' ad campaign. The ads attacked Lorenzo's integrity for clandestinely starting a nonunion airline. To the pilots, Lorenzo was "rotten to the core" (Petzinger 1995). They believed he was creating a sham designed to prohibit Texas International co-pilots from being promoted at New York Air.

## The Proud Bird

Now Lorenzo was ready to make his move on Continental Airlines, "The Proud Bird with the Golden Tail" (Murphy 1986). As usual, he pored over the carrier's financial statements. This probe detected a major disparity between the $290-million value of Continental's fleet and the company's $500-million market value. Next, Lorenzo determined that shares of Continental's common stock were grossly undervalued at $10 a share. Also, Lorenzo believed that institutions holding a large chunk of Continental's shares would be willing to sell if he offered a premium price (Barrett 1987). With his power base established, Lorenzo proposed to Robert Six, Continental's CEO, that the two airlines merge. To Lorenzo's surprise, Six balked (Murphy 1986). But, as usual, Lorenzo had another scheme up his sleeve. As a close friend observed, "[Lorenzo's] secret is not negotiating. He never gets into a situation without an alternative. He tells you straight out what he will do if you don't give him what he wants, and if you don't accept, he will go to Plan B" (Easterbrook 1987, p. 62).

"Plan B" involved accumulating more shares of Continental. When his stock holdings reached roughly 1 million shares, Lorenzo called Six and made a tender offer for Continental. When Six resisted, Lorenzo planned to go directly to other shareholders. However, he failed to anticipate a formidable foe's opposition. Continental's employees declared all-out war against Lorenzo's plan. Their strategy was to leverage their employee stock ownership plan (ESOP).

Paul Eckel, a longtime Continental pilot, organized the Continental Employees Association (CEA) to pursue the counterattack. The ESOP scheme strove to double authorized shares of company stock. This would enable employees to gain at least 51 percent ownership, cutting Lorenzo's position in half, from 48.50 percent to 24.25 percent. The ESOP maneuver would give employees collective ownership of Continental while still allowing each individual to vote his or her personal shares (Murphy 1986).

Sensing the power of opposing forces, Lorenzo took the battle to the New York Stock Exchange (NYSE). The issue concerned the listing of the added ESOP shares. Because Lorenzo's position would be diluted, NYSE rules granted an existing shareholder's power to approve the deal. Lorenzo then disregarded the Civil Aeronautics Board's approval to vote his stock as a block. Knowing no other individual had a larger position, he would prevail.

Bolstered by his victories, Lorenzo had to fight back a last-gasp employee offensive in the California General Assembly. During this intense confrontation, Al Feldman, Continental's CEO, committed suicide. Lorenzo increased his position in Continental to more than 50 percent, thereby completing his political conquest (Barrett 1987).

The turmoil, however, was far from over. When his 1983 appeal for wage concessions from Continental's employees ended up $150 million short, Lorenzo filed for bankruptcy (Ennis 1988). The move was intended to break the union. Bankruptcy notwithstanding, the "New Continental" was back in the skies within seventy-two hours. Its labor costs were now far below those of its competitors. Once again, Lorenzo emerged the victor.

Basking in power, Lorenzo turned his attention to Eastern Airlines, which he eventually acquired. In two short years of ownership, he reduced Eastern's 260-plane fleet by 60, daily flights from 1,500 to 1,000, and the workforce by 13,000 (Bernstein 1990).

Following the same strategy he used at Continental, Lorenzo set out "to rebuild a smaller Eastern and fly it out of bankruptcy" (Bernstein et al. 1989, p. 25). After winning wage concessions from the unions, he sold assets and closed hubs, leaving thousands of Eastern employees jobless (Bernstein 1990). An airline pilots' union president described Lorenzo as having a mind "that would make Machiavelli look like Gomer Pyle" (Schwartz et al. 1989, p. 20).

## Rules? What Rules?

When Lorenzo fought the unions, he negotiated, renegotiated, and then, more often than not, reneged. His pattern was predictable: "His standard bargaining tactic [was] to negotiate a deal as ferociously as possible, haggling over every point in an attempt to wear down his adversary. Then when the other side thought they had an agreement, he would return the next day and say he had forgotten several points" (Bernstein 1990, p. 226). Lorenzo never played by the rules unless they fit his agenda. Even then he changed them when circumstances were not to his liking.

Lorenzo's career was strewn with people mangled in a game of manipulative politics. Not only had his political scheming become a trademark, so too had his political influence. To increase his leverage with federal agencies, Lorenzo, with a shrewd politician's guile, placed high-ranking figures on boards and in top management positions of his companies. He sought allies and formed coalitions with high-stakes players.

When political channels he was trying to use failed to get him what he wanted, Lorenzo simply went around them. The play to get the National Mediation Board (NMB) to start a thirty-day clock so he could force a strike at Eastern is a case in point. Walter Wallace, the NMB chair, favorable to management in past negotiations, quickly became the object of Lorenzo's scorn when he moved too slowly. Lorenzo disregarded Wallace and met with Helen Witt, Wallace's predecessor as head of the mediation board. This maneuver angered the unions, who did not trust Witt, and when Wallace found out about Lorenzo's clandestine attempt, he was infuriated (Bernstein 1990).

Lorenzo's tendency to circumvent people to get his way colored every relationship he formed in the industry. Tom Plaskett, Crandall's understudy at American, was recruited to Continental in November 1986. Plaskett had become enamored of Lorenzo's vision of combining Continental, Eastern, People Express, and Frontier Airlines into the nation's third-largest carrier. However, like others in the revolving door, he lasted a mere seven months. In July 1987 he left and, shortly thereafter, was named president of Pan American. Plaskett never understood Lorenzo's dealings. "He always had an agenda," Plaskett emphasized. "It might be scribbled on a piece of paper, or it might be a formal presentation. One thing was certain; you never knew what his real motives were" (1996).

Another factor that seemed to disturb Plaskett was Lorenzo's inner circle, a close-knit group whose members had bonded as a result of the Continental merger. Plaskett felt that, when major decisions regarding the airline were being made, Lorenzo resorted to this cadre, quietly circumventing him.

## Friendship Airlines: An Oxymoron

When Lorenzo sold his interests in Jet Capital and its successors, Texas Air and Continental Holdings, to Scandinavian Airlines in 1990, the terms of the estimated $20- to $30-million deal included a seven-year noncompetition clause. Lorenzo's promise notwithstanding, within a year of his exit from the industry, he was laying the groundwork for a return. By April 1991, he had formed ATX, a Delaware company in which he and his children owned 74 percent of the stock. Eventually, ATX would become a shell holding company for the proposed Friendship Airlines. But first Lorenzo had to get out of his noncompetition agreement, which he did by paying some $5 million to Continental creditors who had accused him of fraud regarding the sale of his holdings to Scandinavian (O'Brian 1994).

But in this deal Lorenzo's past caught up with him. His request for Department of Transportation certification was challenged by a large coalition of his enemies. The confrontation found its way into the halls of Congress (Ott 1993). There Lorenzo's enemies formed a determined opposition.

## Put on Your Coat

Lorenzo's last chance to get what he wanted came in a courtroom. In his ruling denying Friendship's application, Judge Robert L. Barton Jr. issued several opinions. One, which was a terse response to the way Lorenzo's representatives had conducted themselves in the hearings, stated, "If this is how the Applicant and its personnel behave in a fitness proceeding, when they are seeking a certificate from the Department, and when one could reasonably expect them to be on their best behavior, how will they behave once they have a certificate?" (Bryant 1993, p. D1). This was a veiled reference to the numerous safety violations reported to the Federal Aviation Administration (FAA) regarding airlines formerly operated by Lorenzo.

Continuing his assessment of the hearings, Judge Barton placed little confidence in Lorenzo's testimony, a conclusion based on his "careful observation of the demeanor (including pauses, facial gestures, and body language) of the witness[es]" (Passell 1993, p. D2). Lorenzo and his group failed to display an attitude of respect for the rules. The judge summed up Lorenzo's airline career: "In sum, Mr. Lorenzo's companies have lived on the edge of the law" (Bloomberg 1994, p. D5). An incident that occurred during the proceedings symbolically reflects the judge's perception. On this particular occasion, a hot day in June, Lorenzo took off his coat in the hearing room. Obviously affronted, Judge Barton stopped the proceedings and ordered Lorenzo to put his coat back on. Lorenzo "sheepishly complied" (O'Brian 1994), something he was not accustomed to doing. Once again, as he had at Continental and Eastern, Lorenzo had landed an airline not on a runway but in a courtroom.

## Dancing with His Opposite

Frank Lorenzo can be faulted for many of his manipulative schemes, but if you step back and focus on the ends rather than the means, you see what Lorenzo was able to accomplish in his airline reign. He focused on specific agenda, solidified his power base, built coalitions, neutralized opposition, and was a master of the political game. In the end, his lack of awareness of the consequences of his ruthless tactics did him in. But what might have happened if Lorenzo had been more aware of his shortcomings? What if he had been able to entertain and balance his inner contrary forces?

Nothing reveals Lorenzo's apparent inability to dance with his feminine side more vividly than his long, often tumultuous, relationship with his humanist oppposite, Donald Burr. Burr had supplied Jet Capital (Lorenzo and Carney's venture capital fund) with funds for their takeover of Texas International. Later, Burr joined Lorenzo to form a partnership that took many twists and turns, eventually ending with Burr founding a competing airline: People Express.

After having referred to Burr as "a true soul mate" (Petzinger 1995) and working with him as a top executive, Lorenzo once stopped Burr during a presentation he was making at a board meeting, calling it "complete bullshit." Taking a look at Lorenzo's management-leadership profile reveals a man consumed by facts and figures, which he used as political weapons to attack and acquire struggling airlines. He never seemed to care what happened to the airlines' culture or people. He apparently suppressed his inner humanist and culturist voices and ended up with enterprises that lacked cultural coherence and overlooked human neeeds.

Burr's leaving Lorenzo to found People Express says much about Lorenzo's inability to embrace his humanist and culturist aspects. When Lorenzo suppressed Burr's "bullshit" presentation, he figuratively was suppressing his feminine leanings. Ironically, People Express soon became the fastest-growing airline in aviation history. Had Lorenzo been able to strike a deal with Burr, his mirror opposite, one wonders just how successful an airline they could have built together. The synergy resulting from Lorenzo's analytical and political abilities and Burr's interest in people and culture could have created a powerful force in the industry.

# HILLARY CLINTON:
# A POLITICIST IN THE SENATE

*"It's important to have core principles and values, but if you're going to be active in policy and politics you have to be a realist."*

(Deb's Excellent Conservative Political Pages featuring Rush Limbaugh,

www.dittohead.org, Jan. 22, 2003, p. 3)

As a preschooler, Hillary Rodham Clinton punched a neighborhood bully in the face. Moments later, she rushed home to report, "I can play with the boys now!" (Maraniss 1998, p. 250). She was living up to the name her mother, Dorothy Rodham, had chosen: "Hillary" reflected strength, a name suitable for either a boy or a girl. Years later, as a senator working in the old-boys' chamber, Hillary's contradictory impulses are still evident. "From behind, the silhouette of the freshman senator from New York looks like that of a man. She has been unbound from the ill-fitting bodice of first lady and refitted with long-jacketed pantsuits, allowing her to clasp her hands low, behind the back, in an authoritative military stance" (Sheehy 2001, p. 130).

"Playing with the boys" has developed into a lifelong obsession. Through her partnership with Bill Clinton and now her own political career, Hillary has been able to play with big-time politicians. Her approach to working her way into the Senate was to build coalitions on both sides of the aisle, showing a political savvy that would have made Lyndon Johnson proud. (See Figure 9.)

## Clinton and Clinton: A Partnership of Power

The "Billary" era (Walsh 1998) seems indelibly etched on the nation's psyche. It stems from Bill Clinton's presidential campaign: "When you think of Hillary, think of our real slogan: Buy one, get one free" ("Hillary Rodham Clinton" 1994). The slogan's roots run deep. First as roommates, then as co-prosecutors in their law school's mock trial competition, Bill and Hillary made a formidable team. In a sense, their courtroom partnership was the blueprint for future political partnerships: governor and first lady of

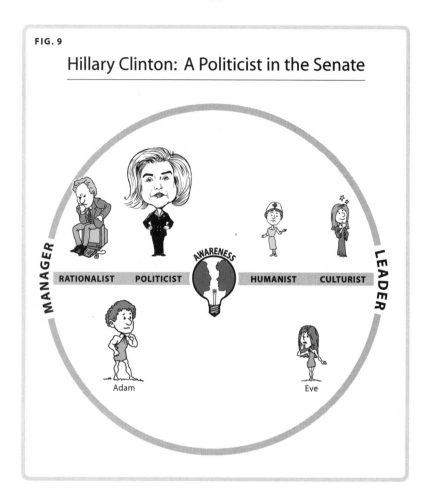

**FIG. 9**

## Hillary Clinton: A Politicist in the Senate

Arkansas, president and first lady of the United States. David Maraniss sums up the political aspirations of Clinton and Clinton: "They realized, they told friends, that they could attain heights together that they might not reach separately" (1998, pp. 76–77). Ironically, their roles reflected "a certain reversal of gender stereotypes" (Maraniss 1995, p. 248).

In *The Case Against Hillary Clinton*, Noonan imagines the shift in history's perspective of Bill Clinton's presidency had Hillary learned to turn the other cheek.

Bill, you were probably no gentleman to Paula—apologize and get this behind us. Bill, later I'll hit you over the head with a frying pan, but for now, tell the truth about that intern; we can't put the country through months of trauma and embarrassment. Bill, I'm handing over the billing papers, and there's something I didn't tell you about Whitewater. Bill, people are walking in here with $50,000 checks and it's against the law and I want it to stop. Bill, I got up for a glass of water last night and there were complete strangers in the Lincoln Bedroom, and if this is how we're raising money then we're doing it wrong. Bill, . . . (2000, p. 164)

Could the trash-the-opposition advice Hillary continually gave her husband be an outgrowth of the early strike-back philosophy her mother instilled (Maraniss 1995, p. 250)?

## Who's the One the Public "Got Free"?

A brilliant legal mind, a female Machiavelli, a children's rights advocate, a woman scorned, a U.S. senator—the person the public got free is a shrewd political operative who claims to be neither a stand-by-your-man woman nor a stay-at-home woman who serves cookies and tea ("Hillary Rodham Clinton" 1994). Hillary wants people to know that "I'm not some ignorant big-hair girl working the counter at the Piggly Wiggly; I went to Yale Law" (Noonan 2000, p. 144). In her book *Living History* (2003), about her experiences in the White House, Hillary attempts to explain her role, one in which she is perceived as being both "co-president" ("Hillary Rodham Clinton" 1994) and "co-scoundrel" (Sheehy 2001).

Bennet describes Hillary's us-versus-them political perspective: "She . . . sees the world in black and white. [Her] politics require villains, be they the entrenched interests of Washington, the insurance companies, or right-wing conspirators. . . . The President's temper scares their advisers, but hers—like a blowtorch . . . *terrifies* them" (1999, p. 26). Hillary's "blowtorch" temper prompted Barbara Olson to title her less than complimentary portrait of Hillary *Hell to Pay* (1999).

# Alinsky to Lewinsky:
# Metamorphosis of an Agenda

Epigraphs derived from *Rules for Radicals* (Saul Alinsky's 1971 how-to blueprint for organizing the poor) introduce chapters of Barbara Olson's indictment of Hillary. A left-wing radical, Alinsky became Hillary's political mentor. But how did "a public enemy of law and order" seduce a young woman who once supported archconservative Barry Goldwater in his bid for the White House? Olson believes "Saul Alinsky taught Hillary to value . . . power" (Olson 1999, pp. 46, 33, 62).

To fulfill Wellesley's graduation requirements, Hillary wrote a thesis, "Aspect[s] of the War on Poverty." The topic grew out of her fascination with Robert Kennedy's interest in the poor. A professor aware of an earlier meeting Hillary had with Alinsky posed the following question: "Why don't you study community organizing and the participation of the poor in Chicago through the Alinsky community?" (Sheehy 1999, p. 66). This ignited Hillary's passion for her controversial research project.

Following Bill Clinton's election, Hillary's alma mater placed her thesis under lock and key. Attempting to explain this action, school officials said, "The undergraduate thesis of any Wellesley graduate or alumna who is or becomes either the President or First Lady of the United States will not be made public" (Sheehy 1999, pp. 66–67). What prompted a policy that obviously applies to only one Wellesley graduate? Olson opines, "Most likely, she does not want the American people to know the extent to which she internalized and assimilated the beliefs and methods of Saul Alinsky" (Olson 1999, p. 46).

Alinsky believed political targets should be polarized (1971, p. 134). This makes it easier to vilify and hence to attack enemies. Once conflict begins, Alinsky says, "the enemy properly goaded and guided in his reaction will be your major strength" (p. 136). When you examine the Clinton administration's scandals, you begin to see how the White House used its enemies' reactions to its own advantage. As manager of the White House "war room,"

Hillary's approach was "to show a balls-out, go-to-the-mat mentality about taking on their enemies. Anybody who has a hang-up
about fairness is cast out as part of the enemy camp" (Olson 1999,
p. 209).

Hillary's take-no-prisoners style weaves its way from one White
House scandal to another. When she and Clinton appeared on *60
Minutes* to explain the Gennifer Flowers affair, Hillary seized control. Her attention to such details as the height of chairs and the positions she and Clinton occupied on the set prompted Steve Kroft to
say, "If you didn't know she was his wife, you'd have thought she
was a media consultant" (Olson 1999, p. 212).

Throughout major crises—Whitewater, Filegate, Travelgate,
Vince Foster's tragic suicide, and eventually the Monica Lewinsky
affair—Hillary continued to mastermind White House defenses. In
the Lewinsky situation, her defense was that her husband's problems with women stemmed in part from his being torn between his
mother and his grandmother. This tack apparently harmonizes with
what Clinton told ABC's Carol Simpson. When asked what historians would say about his affair with Lewinsky, he replied, "They
will say I made a bad personal mistake, and I paid a serious price
for it, but that I was right to stand and fight for my country, my
constitution, and its principles" (Simpson 1999).

Hillary's denials appear to echo Alinsky's admonitions to un-
cover, reveal wrongdoings, and disprove competency allegations.
Even after her husband admitted on national television that he had
misled her in his relationship with Monica, Hillary took initiative
in a way that would have made Alinsky proud. First, she personified the enemy as a "vast right-wing conspiracy" out to get her husband. Then, taking another cue from *Rules for Radicals,* she
provoked her adversaries, believing, "You can club them to death
with their 'book' of rules and regulations" (Alinsky 1971, p. 152).

Hillary and Bill constantly stretch opinions of judges and pros-
ecutors beyond reasonable interpretation. Recall, "It depends on
what *is* is." William Safire's insightful analysis of Hillary's style appears to hit the mark: "Americans of all political persuasions are

coming to the sad realization that our first lady—a woman of undoubted talents who was a role model for many in her generation—is a congenital liar" (Safire 1996, p. 27).

## Senator Clinton

In high school, Hillary Rodham told a reporter for the school paper that she wanted "to marry a senator and settle down in Georgetown" ("Hillary Rodham Clinton" 1994). Most people would dismiss this as a teenager's passing fancy. Yet history proves that Hillary Clinton should never be taken lightly. Rather than marry a senator, she married a man who would become president and currently lives in Georgetown as the junior senator from New York.

In its endorsement of Clinton's Senate candidacy, the *New York Times* projects she will be able to lay aside the baggage she brings.

> The investigative literature of Whitewater and related scandals is replete with evidence that Mrs. Clinton has a lamentable tendency to treat political opponents as enemies. She has clearly been less than truthful in her comments to investigators and too eager to follow President Clinton's method of peddling access for campaign donations. Her fondness for stonewalling in response to legitimate questions about financial or legislative matters contributed to the bad ethical reputation of the Clinton administration. ("Hillary Clinton for the Senate" 2000, p. 14)

Recognizing her opponent's attempt "to exploit the carpetbagger issue" (Clinton is not a native of the state), the *Times* defends its support by concluding that "Mrs. Clinton is capable of growing beyond the ethical legacies of her Arkansas and White House years" (p. 14). A member of a Capitol Hill prayer group, observing Hillary in the Senate, sums up the *Times'* prophetic assessment: "You have to hand it to that Hillary. . . . She may be wicked, but she's effective" (Sheehy 2001, p. 177).

Only days before her swearing in, Hillary found herself embroiled in yet another controversy. She signed an $8 million book deal for the rights to her memoirs. Immediately, detractors accused her of consummating the deal prior to entering office to avoid any ethical conflict with Senate rules. After taking the oath, Clinton offered to support rules that would prohibit future book deals. Critics compared her deal to that of Newt Gingrich. He was forced to return a reported $4 million for rights to his memoirs. Hillary supporters countered by saying Gingrich's contract was negotiated privately. Hillary's, they claimed, resulted from the dynamics of competing market forces.

As Clinton entered the Senate and her husband exited the presidency, issues continued to arise in what has been described as a shameless endgame. The pardon of financier Marc Rich and the appropriation of White House furniture were part of the later moves on a chessboard where the Clintons were often trapped but never checkmated. Rich, a fugitive since 1983, owes the government an estimated $48 million in taxes on some $100 million he amassed while trading with enemies of the United States. According to the Clintons, the White House furniture was taken in error.

## Building Coalitions

Scandals notwithstanding, Clinton approaches the Senate with the skills of a seasoned politicist. Coalition building and power are her means, pursuing agenda her end. Clinton's name has already appeared on hundreds of Senate bills. She attributes this to "many of my colleagues [recognizing] that sometimes they can get more attention if I'm involved" (Kiely 2001, p. A8). But does "the coyness of her soft words [belie] the hardness of her deeds" (Olson 1999, p. 3)? Shrewdly, Hillary is attempting to blend the styles of former New York senators Moynihan and Amato. Moynihan was a big-picture liberal, Amato a pothole conservative. "I want to be a big-picture pothole senator," she says (Kiely 2001, p. A8). Republican stalwarts Orrin Hatch and Arlen Specter offer their praises:

"Let me tell you, it's been a wonderful thing to work with her," beams Hatch, and Specter adds, "She has a distinguished career ahead. . . . What's happened in the past is not even a prologue" (Sheehy 2001, p. 178).

Is Clinton using senators the way her detractors accuse her of using children's rights? She believes children, regardless of age, should be allowed to speak for themselves. Carried to the extreme, one writer believes, this opens the door "for ventriloquists to speak through them and thus to disguise their own objectives as the child's" (Christopher Larch in Noonan 2000, p. 151).

As first lady, Hillary often spoke through her husband. Now, she says, "I'm speaking for myself." Yet she is promoting a political agenda not unlike that of the Clinton White House: "a proliferation of state-managed and taxpayer-funded programs" (p. 151). Recall that as co-president she designed, managed, and attempted to market a 1,364-page health-care program that covered all Americans (Bennet 1999). It failed because "[Hillary] had a tin ear for how to sell her ideas" (Sheehy 1999, p. 241). Ironically, she promoted her New York campaign as a "listening tour."

In her campaign, Hillary convinced New Yorkers that she knew what was best. A close aide present in many of those sessions describes Hillary's self-righteous style: "She got defensive very quickly. So it came across as 'I know better. I have higher standards. I have better ideals. I have bigger plans.' One gets the feeling that Hillary thinks she is better than you are" (p. 241).

In building coalitions, Hillary seems to know whom to seek out. Just as Lyndon Johnson aligned himself with Richard Russell when he entered the Senate, Hillary went after Robert Byrd, one of the chamber's longest-serving members (Sheehy 2001). Cozying up to Byrd is Hillary's way of paying respect, or showing humility, and being politically correct. Later, when suggesting to Tom Daschle that a war room was needed to thwart Republican efforts, the majority leader reminded her that Senate battles are not fought hand-to-hand.

Hillary's status among "the boys" is on the rise. Initially, her office was located in the basement of the Russell building, like most freshman senators. Now she occupies the top-floor office of the late senator Patrick Moynihan. The move raised eyebrows; there were ninety-eight senators ahead of Hillary in seniority. Ironically, her office is next to Trent Lott's, former leader of Senate Republicans.

No woman in recent history understands what it takes to be a successful politician better than Hillary Clinton. She's been mentored by her husband, arguably one of the best politicians in history. But what will she bring to the Senate from the Clinton and Clinton partnership, and what baggage will she cast aside?

Hillary undoubtedly will attempt to distance herself from scandals. But the fact that she once participated and tried to put a spin on negative details with the passion of a defense attorney will be a hard legacy to overcome. Many Americans do not trust Hillary and never will. She needs a new image. As one writer says, "The best refuge for a co-scoundrel is the Senate—where they take very seriously the concept of courtesy" (Sheehy 2001, p. 178). When Hillary's charm unites with the protective spirit of male senators, a new persona may evolve. Hillary may become her own person, one whose multiple political and interpersonal talents will be put to good use.

Hillary is an outstanding lawyer; her legal skills will be a tremendous political advantage in crafting legislation to support her agenda for New York. She is able to raise enormous amounts of money. Already the success of her political action committee, HillPAC, is placing her in a position of power among Democrats (Kiely 2001, p. A8). *It Takes a Village,* her book on raising children, cements her abilities as a gifted writer. She is able to express her ideas in a candid fashion. She is an accomplished orator. Her hard-knocks experience as first lady in Arkansas and Washington have toughened her. She will not run from a political fight, regardless of the opponent. All in all, she will be a successful senator who knows what she wants and knows how to get it.

## Dancing with Her Opposite

We witnessed "a certain reversal of gender stereotypes" during Bill Clinton's presidency, and many Americans see it now as they recognize the powerful role Hillary continues to play. Dancing with her opposite appears to come naturally to Hillary, but are appearances deceiving?

Answers to this question pose new questions. Does Hillary use children to achieve her political agenda? How involved was she in the scandals surrounding her husband's presidency? Is she a carpetbagger senator, or is she genuinely interested in the people of New York? One's perspective notwithstanding, Hillary Clinton stands out as a tough politicist. Those who cross her have "hell to pay." Ironically, Hillary seems more at home in roles generally associated with men than those generally associated with women. Can we conclude that, as with most men, her Eve is suppressed? Are her political leanings balanced with concern for peoples' needs, rational analysis, and cultural sensitivities? Is she aware of her strong points and her weaknesses?

When Bill Clinton campaigned for the presidency, he told Americans they were getting two for the price of one. Did he mean two *presidents*? Will Hillary become the second Clinton—and, more significantly, the first woman—to occupy the Oval Office? Many signs seem to point in that direction.

If success in the Senate is any indication, Hillary's chances of becoming the nation's first female president are very good. Even her adversaries view her political savvy as second only to that of her husband, whom many believe to be one of the best politicians in history. Both friend and foe predict Hillary will seek, and quite possibly win, the Democratic Party's nomination. One would be well advised not to sell her short. She is tough, smart, and as adept at navigating Washington's labyrinthine halls as any senator or congressional representative who has ever entered those venerable institutions. Her Republican opponent will be in for the fight of his life, one he might well lose.

# LYNDON JOHNSON:
# A POLITICIST IN THE PRESIDENCY

*"I do understand power, whatever else may be said about me.*
*I know where to look for it, and how to use it."*

(Caro 2002, p. xx)

Lyndon Baines Johnson assumed the presidency following John Kennedy's assassination. He then articulated a broad, albeit pragmatic, agenda. "When I first became president, I realized that if only I could take the next step and become dictator of the whole world, then I could really make things happen" (Kearns 1976, p. 194). Establishing the "Great Society" was the centerpiece of what Johnson wanted to make happen. As he put it, "I want to be president of all the people. . . . I want for every family what my mother wanted for me: the chance for an honest living, an honorable job, a decent future" ("LBJ" 1991).

"To free 30 million Americans from the prison of poverty," Johnson knew he needed a broad base of power, one that would secure support for an avalanche of legislation. Toward this end, his vast experience in Congress served him well. Close friend and political confidant John Connally described Johnson as having "a talent for attaching himself to power." Johnson's relationship with Richard Russell is a case in point. When he entered the Senate, Johnson quickly recognized the influence the Georgia senator wielded among his colleagues. So enamored was Johnson of Russell, an aide jokingly said that if Russell had been a woman Johnson would have married him. Johnson is firmly positioned on the left in Figure 10.

On more than one occasion during his congressional years, Johnson could be found in cloakrooms wheeling and dealing, attempting to manipulate those he sought to control. "He seemed to possess a wholly intuitive ability to perceive a man's nature so accurately and profoundly as almost to be unnatural" (Kearns 1976, p. 372). Johnson specialized in knowing his colleagues' Achilles' heels. The "weaknesses," "vulnerabilities," "prides," and "fears" formed "a virtual encyclopedia of the fallibility of his fellow legisla-

**FIG. 10**

## Lyndon Johnson: A Politicist in the Presidency

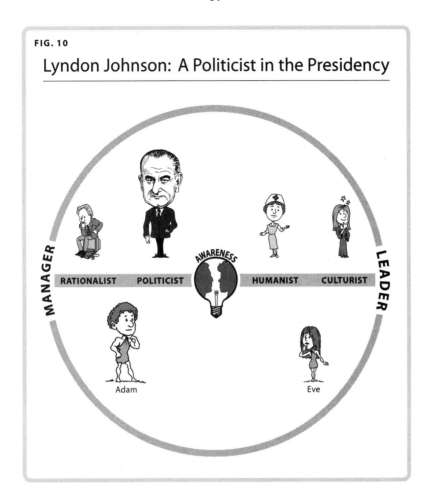

tors" (Barber 1992, p. 73). In *Master of the Senate,* Robert Caro amplifies the views of Kearns and Barber:

> He had a genius for studying a man and learning his strengths and weaknesses and hopes and fears . . . what it was that the man wanted—not what he said he wanted but what he really wanted—and what it was that the man feared, really feared. (Caro 2002, p. 136)

Johnson's knowledge of his Senate colleagues was one of the tools he used to become "the youngest Minority Leader (44)" and "the youngest Majority Leader (46) in the history of the United States" (Caro 2002, p. 557). Once he had gained control, Johnson "transformed the United States Senate—remade that body, seemingly so immutable, in his own image. He could run it now, run it as he wanted to run it" (Caro 2002, p. 580).

As his career moved from the Senate to the vice presidency, and ultimately to the presidency, Johnson amassed power with unmatched fervor and guile. Derisively referred to as "Landslide Lyndon," he had won his Senate seat by a meager eighty-seven votes in a race many accused him of stealing (Kearns 1976). Assuming the presidency after Kennedy was assassinated did not help his image. Nevertheless, Johnson embarked on a mission to prove that he was legitimate regardless of what the Eastern Establishment thought ("LBJ" 1991). Many perceived Johnson to be a "political virtuoso," an FDR "New Deal" liberal who could "out-right" the most conservative of conservatives. Perhaps their perception stemmed from what one aide described as a Johnson trick of the trade: "Lyndon Johnson knew that the illusion of power was almost as important as real power itself, that, simply the more powerful you appeared to be, the more powerful you became. It was one of the reasons for his great success" (Caro 2002, p. 596).

Described by one associate as a Jekyll and Hyde, Johnson, at the flip of a switch, could change from a seemingly warm, backslapping friend into a cold, manipulating foe. Early on, his mother had taught him that power should be used for the benefit of people rather than for one's own purposes. His "Jekyll" inspired him to seek prosperity for every American, while his "Hyde" seduced him into sending young Americans to Vietnam.

## Johnson's Style

"An emphasis on personal relations" is how one writer describes Johnson's style (Barber 1992, p. 66). But "personal relations," the stock-in-trade of politicists, should not be confused with human relations, the stock-in-trade of humanists. Through personal relations, a politicist builds coalitions that help implement his agenda.

Here the focus is on what others can contribute to the politicist's end. Through human relations, a humanist attempts to meet the needs of people. Here the focus is on others' needs. Self-interest tends to motivate many politicians, while other-interest tends to motivate most humanists.

Roots of Johnson's shrewdness in personal dealings reach back to his early years. While a student at tiny San Marcos College, he worked his way through numerous jobs, finally landing a plum position—he became special assistant to the president's secretary. Johnson turned a menial job into a source of power. College personnel quickly learned that to get to the president they had to go through Johnson (Kearns 1976, p. 48).

As a young legislative assistant in Washington, Johnson continued to exploit the power he was discovering in personal relations. At the hotel where most of the assistants stayed, he took four showers the first night and brushed his teeth five times the following morning. Spacing his visits to the bathroom he shared with his peers allowed Johnson to meet more people quickly.

By the time he entered the White House, Johnson had perfected what came to be known as the "Johnson treatment" ("LBJ" 1991). Arthur Schlesinger Jr. described what it was like to experience Johnson's magnetism:

> The treatment began immediately: a brilliant, capsule characterization of every Democratic Senator: his strengths and failings; where he fit into the political spectrum; how far he could be pushed, how far pulled; his hates, his loves. And who ([Johnson] asked Schlesinger) must oversee all these prima donnas, put them to work, knit them together, know when to tickle this one's vanity, inquire of that one's health, remember this one's five o'clock nip of Scotch, that one's nagging wife? Who must find the hidden legislative path between the South and the North, the public power men and the private power men, the farmer's men and the union's men, the bomber-boys and the peace lovers, the eggheads and the fatheads? Nobody but Lyndon Johnson. (in Barber 1992, pp. 66–67)

Encounters with Johnson "were like standing under a water-fall" ("LBJ" 1991). At times flattery flowed; at times you became the target of abuse. Depending on how a particular individual fit his agenda, Johnson played three distinct roles. Was the person someone Johnson needed? Did Johnson already control him? Or was he no longer of any political value? (Barber 1992). Johnson's agenda was akin to a coach's game plan: The person he needed was a "recruit"; the person he controlled was a "current player"; and anyone who had left was an "ex-player."

### The Recruit

A White House meeting with the late Everett Dirksen pictures Johnson horse-trading with the Illinois senator. White House aide Jack Valenti narrates the conversation:

> *Johnson:* Everett, I wouldn't talk about a cur dog the way you did me in the Senate.
> *Dirksen:* Well, Mr. President, I vow to tell the truth; I have no choice.
> *Johnson, handing Dirksen a list of votes he needs:* Now, Everett, I got to have three Republican votes, and you know who they are, and I don't want any beating around the bush.
> *Dirksen, pulling a list out of his pocket:* Well, Mr. President, I happen to have here some names of some likely nominees to the Federal Power Commission and the Federal Communications Commission and some other commissions.
> *Johnson:* Give those names to Valenti. ("LBJ" 1991)

Out of this exchange, Johnson got three votes and Dirksen got three appointees to federal commissions.

### The Current Player

When Johnson already controlled a person, he could be brutal. A tirade unleashed at Valenti illustrates the point. "I thought I told you, Jack, to fix this f—— doorknob!" "Where the g—— hell ya bin?" "How many times have I got to tell you not to leave your office without telling me where you're going?" "For Chrissake, do you spend all your time on the phone?" (Barber 1992, p. 68)

### The Ex-Player

Johnson was less than gracious in his comments about two key aides after they left his staff. When Bill Moyers left the White House, Johnson said, "When [he] became my Press Secretary, my popularity was at an all-time high and nobody ever heard of Bill Moyers. When he left I was at an all-time low and Bill Moyers was a world hero" (Barber 1992, p. 70).

When longtime aide Bobby Baker became the subject of a Senate investigation, Johnson went public with his opinion that the Senate was "conducting [an] investigation of an employee of theirs—no protégé of anyone; he was there before I came to the Senate for ten years, doing the same job as he is doing now; he was elected by all the senators . . . including the Republican senators" (p. 70). Baker had developed a reputation as "Little Lyndon" and often boasted, "I have ten senators in the palm of my hand" ("LBJ" 1991).

Charming when he needed people and cruel when he didn't, Johnson promised people the Great Society and delivered many of its promised programs. His power of persuasion was a two-edged sword. When Johnson used power positively, it became his greatest strength. When he used power negatively, it became his greatest weakness. He charmed people into believing that the Great Society was in plain sight and deceived them into believing that a win in Vietnam was around the corner.

## The Great Society

Johnson referred to the Great Society as "the woman I really loved" (Kearns 1976, p. 251). But who was this woman and why did Johnson hold her in such high regard? The "woman" was

Johnson's metaphor for what he envisioned society becoming. "When she grew up," he said, "I figured she'd be so big and beautiful that the American people couldn't help but fall in love with her . . . making her a permanent part of American life" (p. 286). Full grown, this "woman" had something to offer every American:

> Medicare for the old, educational assistance for the young, tax rebates for business, a higher minimum wage for labor, subsidies for farmers, vocational training for the unskilled, food for the hungry, housing for the homeless, poverty grants for the poor, clean highways for commuters, legal protection for the blacks, improved schooling for the Indians, rehabilitations for the lame, higher benefits for the unemployed, reduced quotas for the immigrants, auto safety for the driver, pensions for the retired, fair labeling for consumers, conservation for the hikers and the campers. . . . (p. 216)

Immediately following his landslide victory over Goldwater, Johnson began laying the groundwork for his Great Society. This involved pushing a bewildering number of bills through Congress. To get his agenda moving, Johnson drew on two favorite sources of power—his knowledge of the legislative process and his genius at persuading people. "If it's really going to work," he said, "the relationship between the President and the Congress has got to be almost incestuous. He's got to know them even better than they know themselves" (p. 226). Indeed, Johnson did.

But understanding people was one thing, and understanding himself was another. Past successes had taught Johnson that willpower could overcome almost anything. Building a great society at home and managing a war thousands of miles away were but two obstacles that could be overcome with his powerful will. In the language of economics, he determined to produce "guns and butter" at the same time. Making butter was not difficult in a growing economy. But as the need for guns siphoned scarce resources, the conflict between butter and guns caused problems.

# The Vietnam War

With the same passion with which he embraced the Great Society as "the woman [he] really loved," Johnson spurned Vietnam as "that bitch of a war" (Kearns 1976, p. 251). But how did the beloved society eventually become lost in the shadow of the bitch war? Like Nixon, Johnson was consumed with how the American people perceived him. Did they see him as being tough on communism? He feared they did not when Barry Goldwater questioned his patriotism in the 1964 presidential campaign. To dispel tormenting doubts, Johnson embarked on a disastrous course. He increased America's presence in a war that would eventually eat away the foundations of the Great Society.

Martin Luther King Jr. observed Johnson's dilemma through a pragmatic lens: "The bombs in Vietnam [are exploding] at home. They [are destroying] the dream and possibility for a decent America" ("LBJ" 1991). King figured that it cost $322,000 to kill one enemy soldier and only $53 to deliver one American from the grip of poverty.

Johnson's reasoning, though questionable, was simultaneously magnanimous and selfish. Magnanimously, he convinced Americans that it was better to contain communism in Southeast Asia than on America's West Coast. Selfishly, he politically wanted to move from the long shadow cast by John Kennedy. If he won in Vietnam, he would "out-Kennedy" Kennedy. After all, it was Kennedy's war and he had not been able to end it. Many believed Johnson used the Gulf of Tonkin Resolution, even though its claims were questionable if not outright false, to give him the unlimited power he needed to bring Ho Chi Minh to his knees. Johnson "saw our bombs as political resources for negotiating peace" ("LBJ" 1991).

Jack Valenti, Johnson's right-hand man, likened escalation in Vietnam to a bottle of olives: "pulling out the first one was difficult, but the second and third came easier and easier" ("LBJ" 1991). Slowly, Johnson deceived himself and the American people. As he stepped up the bombing, he "thought the war would be like a filibuster—enormous resistance at first, then a steady whittling away, then Ho hurrying to get it over with" (David McCullough in "LBJ" 1991). But Ho Chi Minh was not a United States senator. For once, Johnson could not rely on his powers of persuasion. Throughout his life, he had been convinced his "treatment" would work on anyone. If only he could look them in the eye, he would convince them of what was in their "best interests." Further, he was sure that once Ho Chi Minh surrendered, he could get Congress to pour $1 billion into Vietnam and reproduce his Great Society there as well ("LBJ" 1991). Sadly, he failed on both fronts. The man who entered the White House saying he had never felt freer was finding out what many of his predecessors had learned: It was like a prison.

## "My Fellow Americans"

When Lyndon Johnson won the 1964 presidential election, he immediately set out to secure equality for all his "fellow Americans." He confided to an aide, "I'm going to be the president who finishes what Lincoln began" ("LBJ" 1991). When the Civil Rights Act of 1964 became law, he did finish something that Lincoln had started a hundred years earlier. But Johnson went further. Addressing members of Congress in 1965 on national television, he challenged them to pass the Voting Rights Act, punctuating his address with "we shall overcome," words from the hymn associated with Martin Luther King Jr. and the Civil Rights movement.

As Johnson's legislative successes grew (he kept a scorecard in his pocket), he imagined himself becoming one of the great presidents in history. He and his Great Society were being compared to Roosevelt and his New Deal. He had horse-traded his way to the summit of political power, a position he began coveting early when his mother convinced him that power could and should be used to benefit mankind. But, seemingly in a moment, the man who had been described by Hubert Humphrey as a political giant discovered that he had feet of clay.

Why could he not bring himself to admit that Vietnam was an unwinnable war? The answer seems to be Johnson's lust for power. He failed to heed the wisdom of Lord Acton: Power tends to corrupt, and absolute power corrupts absolutely. Through repeated misrepresentation of U.S. involvement in Vietnam, Johnson maintained absolute control over the conduct of the war. But, as the fighting escalated, Johnson found himself in circumstances he could not control. Vietnam was not the U.S. Senate. Controlling soldiers thousands of miles from home was not the same as controlling a hundred senators in one-on-one meetings.

Yet Johnson, ever the manipulator, attempted to build coalitions of a different sort. His taped telephone conversations reveal calls to former presidents Truman and Eisenhower in which he sought their approval of decisions he had already made. He then would leak the conversations to the press to spread the word that both former presidents supported his decisions. Other phone calls reveal a man so desperate for public approval that, shortly after the assassination of John Kennedy, he toyed with the idea of appointing Jackie the nation's ambassador to Mexico. Such behind-the-scenes antics provoked a television commentator to describe Johnson as "scheming and manipulating . . . devious . . . with the American people" (Stahl 2001).

As the war continued, Johnson lost control of the press and, in turn, his fellow Americans. They realized he had been lying to them all along. The man whose ego was so big that his initials "LBJ" adorned his shirts, his ranch, his wife (Lady Bird Johnson), his daughters (Luci Baines Johnson and Lynda Bird Johnson), and his dog (Little Beagle Johnson) refused to accept reality. His refusal motivated satirists to lampoon the once powerful LBJ.

In the 1967 play *Macbird*, Barbara Garson tells LBJ's story, recasting him as Shakespeare's Macbeth. Overly harsh in its satirical suggestion that Johnson was behind John Kennedy's assassination, *Macbird* did magnify a trait Johnson shared with his Shakespearean counterpart. While Johnson and Macbeth were capable of reaching great heights, they were equally capable of sinking to even greater depths—their self-destruction (Jones 2002). In Johnson's case, many of the Great Society's triumphs ended in the tragedy of Vietnam.

## Dancing with His Opposite

Few would deny Lyndon Johnson his place among the nation's great politicists. Yet many would argue with some of his policies, particularly the decision to escalate America's involvement in Vietnam. This decision eventually overshadowed his determination to establish a Great Society, and that it did underscores Johnson's inability to dance with his opposite.

Think of the Great Society as representing Johnson's more feminine, humanist side and of Vietnam as his more masculine, politicist side. Now Johnson's internal struggles come into focus. Sadly, the war apparently forced his humanist side off the dance floor.

## THREE PROFILES, ONE STYLE

Now that you have seen profiles of three people who favor a political approach, reflect on your own management style. Do you recognize yourself in the management styles of Lorenzo, Clinton, or Johnson? Consider their styles, not their personalities.

- Does your sense of things lead you to sources of power?
- Are you a coalition builder?
- Do you recognize the importance of controlling limited resources?

If you answer yes, then the politicist may personify your dominant style. Let's review the position each person occupies on our continuum.

### Lorenzo

Even though Lorenzo's analytical abilities played an important role in his career, his caricature is dominated by the politicist's drive for power. Politicists recognize that resources are limited. To implement their agenda, they build coalitions to broaden their power base. Politicists tend to be dominated by their Adam, and their Eve is often suppressed. In our view, Lorenzo's Adam dwarfs his Eve.

In Lorenzo's style, one detects some rationalist aspects but even more politicist. His humanist and culturist side is quite small. As pointed out, Lorenzo lacked empathy for people. Symbolically, when Burr departed Texas International, the vision of a human relations department at Texas International left with him.

## Clinton

One finds Clinton's caricature to the left of center, dominated by her politicist leanings. Yet one cannot deny that her style, like Lorenzo's, has a strong rationalist component. From the time she punched the neighborhood bully, to the time she formed a partnership with Bill Clinton, to the time she entered the Senate, Hillary Clinton focused on one main goal: acquiring power. Note how we see the size of her Adam as compared to her Eve.

Reviewing Clinton's profile, we see a woman who created a war room in the White House, whose sole purpose was to attack and discredit her husband's enemies. As one writer pointed out, cross Hillary and you have "hell to pay." The fact that she has dodged both personal and political scandals underscores her well-honed Machiavellian instincts. She seems to be more at ease in her Adam-dominated drive for power than in her Eve's concern for the reputation and welfare of others.

## Johnson

Like the caricatures of Lorenzo and Clinton, we locate Johnson's on the model's left side, dominated by his strong politicist leanings. Arguably, few in the history of American politics have been more adept at building coalitions than Johnson. Through his skill at developing personal relations, he gathered power as few before or after have done. This is why we conclude his Adam dominates his Eve.

But recall that Johnson was driven by his vision to establish a Great Society, a passion he spoke of as loving a woman. Thus his humanist side was not far from the surface. Yet he could not disentangle himself from the war in Vietnam. When push came to shove, Johnson reverted to his more masculine politicist leanings.

Regardless of how you view Lorenzo, Clinton, and Johnson, they are highly successful individuals in their respective worlds of business and politics. But could they be even more successful by learning to dance with their opposites? Remember our admonition that politics can be a positive game, one in which, at one time or another, we all become involved as either players or spectators. The character of the politicist determines how and for whom he or she plays the game. If the politicist profiles do not speak to you, read on. Perhaps you will identify with either the humanist or the culturist profiles appearing in the following chapters.

# The Humanist

**human resource**
## Humanist
**Feeling**

Humanists champion people, facilitate meeting personal needs, and work to liberate human potential. They are supportive and encourage participation. Two separate but related assumptions dominate the humanist approach: The first is that personal needs are carried along when people come to work, so the leader's job is to create a supportive work environment in which personal needs can be satisfied. The second is that people have sound ideas about how to make improvements, and, by providing people with opportunities to participate in important discussions, a company enriches its ability to learn and grow. Learning organizations are an outgrowth of this community-building philosophy.

Humanists go to great lengths to make sure the results of decisions harmonize with the participative environment they champion. This explains their use of the collective "we" rather than the individual "I."

In contrast to rationalists, who critique people's performance to increase efficiency, humanists encourage people. A rationalist poses questions such as, Are we measuring their performance? Why aren't they more productive? What are the costs? How does it affect the bottom line? Can it be made more efficiently? Humanists emphasize: Our people are the best in the industry. They take pride in what they do. As long as everyone is pulling together, they don't care who gets the credit. A person's individual growth is just as highly valued as his or her contribution to the bottom line. Humanists see people as individuals, not as parts of the machinery of production.

How do humanists harmonize needs of individuals with organizational goals? The following profiles of three humanist leaders—former People Express CEO Donald Burr, women's movement pioneer Betty Friedan, and former president Jimmy Carter—offer food for thought. Each seems more comfortable in the role of humanist than in the role of rationalist, politicist, or culturist.

# DONALD BURR:
# A HUMANIST IN BUSINESS

*"[W]e take care of each other. And we take care of customers.*
*Within those bounds, you can do just about anything."*
(Gendron 1985, p. 28)

As a young boy, Donald Burr exhibited oratorical skills that belied his age. He often used his powers of persuasion to convince his parents that a weekend jaunt to Hartford's nearby airport was in everyone's best interest. Very early, he became enamored of airplane landings and takeoffs. In his imagination, the planes were flying to new horizons, toward a world where people might live and work together in harmony. Burr later reflected on these early dreams in a news interview, "I always liked aviation. It's romantic. It's the moon; it's the beyond; it's questing. It's not toilet paper. In aviation there's the hidden promise that there's something better out there

FIG. 11

Donald Burr: A Humanist in Business

somewhere" (Aronoff and Ward 1992, p. 66). In boyhood, the stage was set for Burr's founding of People Express. His airline quickly became the fastest-growing endeavor in aviation history.

As a Stanford undergraduate, Burr was drawn to the business world (Ramsey 1987). The yearning flew in the face of his upbringing. His religious parents had once admonished him that "Business is dirty and bad. . . . You'll certainly not be a businessman" (Petzinger 1995, p. 41). Burr took the seamy route anyway, switching his major from English to economics (Ramsey 1987). Yet he never lost his humanistic bearings. Figure 11 depicts his profile.

## Burr Meets Lorenzo

Burr pursued his education at Harvard Business School. Following graduation he became a security analyst with National Aviation (Byrne 1985). There he learned the financial intricacies of the airline industry, rubbing shoulders with chief executives as well as investment bankers. On one occasion, he was introduced to Frank Lorenzo, a venture capitalist looking for airline investment opportunities (Petzinger 1995). Burr and Lorenzo later developed a complex, stormy relationship, described by some as "cosmic" (Plaskett 1996). Early on, Burr thought he had Lorenzo figured out. He discovered later that he was wrong. When Lorenzo asked him to join Texas International, Burr understood that he would become co–chief executive. Al Feldman, Frontier Airline's chairman, observed in Lorenzo's presence that Burr's business card identified him as head of Texas International's executive committee, the airline's top position. Lorenzo took note. Upon returning to Texas International's Houston headquarters, Burr learned about his corrected title: Lorenzo had demoted him from co–chief executive to executive vice president (Petzinger 1995).

In spite of such periodic transgressions, the personal bond between the corporate "odd couple" persevered. Burr was the best man in Lorenzo's wedding and later asked Lorenzo to be his son's godfather. Though not one to show emotion, Lorenzo confided to friends that Burr was "a true soul mate" (p. 96).

## Opposites at Texas International

Burr argued that Texas International should emphasize low fares and human relations. This strategy, he believed, would determine whether the airline would prevail in the competitive air wars following deregulation. Burr wanted a "People University," resembling Southwest Airlines' training center, as a centerpiece for achieving a personalized work environment in which employees cared about each other and worked voluntarily to achieve company goals. Burr prepared his humanist case for the company's board with the precision of a trial lawyer. He believed he could demonstrate that "every 1 percent increase in business attributable to newly happy and productive employees . . . would be worth $1,441,660 of additional revenue to the company" (Petzinger 1995, p. 98). With this ideal front and center, he was ready to make his presentation to top executives.

During the meeting, Burr got a dose of Lorenzo's wrath. A few minutes into the presentation, Lorenzo interrupted Burr and summoned him to his office. "This is complete bullshit," Lorenzo caustically bellowed (p. 98). Lorenzo's response devastated Burr and severed the relationship between the two. Within a year, Burr launched his own airline, a venture that would reflect his humanist philosophy.

## Six Precepts

Burr's philosophy was condensed into six guiding precepts or objectives that evolved from meetings of People Express officers. These were the ideals (Petzinger 1995, pp. 119–120; Whitestone and Schlesinger 1995, p. 5):

1. Service—commitment to the growth and development of our people; taking care of our people

2. To be the best provider of air transportation; taking care of our customers better than any other airline

3. To provide the highest quality of leadership

4. To serve as a role model for others

5. Simplicity

6. Maximization of profits

With unbridled passion, Burr sought to imprint these six principles on the heart of every People Express employee. However, he believed "the overarching purpose of People's Express" stemmed from the first two precepts: taking care of our people and taking care of our customers. Realizing these two "people" precepts automatically led to the carrier's ultimate purpose: "[to] become the leading institution for constructive change in the world" (Holland and Beer 1993, p. 4).

## Burr's Humanist Church

People Express became Burr's "humanist church," reconciling a desire to own an airline with an equally important zeal to serve people. By combining the humanistic fervor of People's first five precepts with the realistic sixth—making a profit—Burr was convinced he could balance human ideals with a healthy bottom line. His airline would then be seen as a model. It would be an enterprise whose precepts would be the building blocks for constructing a better world.

With evangelistic fervor, Burr outlined his philosophy to students at the Harvard Business School. He portrayed authoritarian managers as the true enemies of corporate progress. In his eyes, these automatons stuffed people into boxes and instilled in them a no-sir, yes-sir military mind-set. In a mock role-play before the students, Burr dramatized his point. He facetiously ordered one of the students to "go outside and kill yourself and when you get back I'll tell you what to do next." Following the simulation, he outlined People Express' strategy for eradicating such cretinlike management tactics.

People's strategy empowered employees so they, in turn, could transform both workplace and world. To reach these lofty goals, Burr devised a three-step process: First, he laid out a decentralized organizational structure, resolving the conflict between freedom and control by freeing rather than oppressing people. Second, he created a caring context that encouraged each employee to take a proprietary interest in People Express and its people. Third, he encouraged employees to model the company's values by sharing their newfound faith with the airline's passengers.

Employee meetings became emotion-packed forums for conveying the spirit of the company's precepts. Sessions often ended with a Pygmalion-like challenge from Burr: "You're not a commodity. The minute you think you're a commodity you'll end up an undifferentiated mass—bubble gum on the streets. You're not a beaten-down worker. You're a manager. You're an owner" (Rimer 1984, p. 29).

Believing the road to profits was achieved through caring about people, Burr frequently condensed the message to "You have two parameters at People Express: Take care of people; take care of customers. How could you be more free?" Burr continued, "Make all the mistakes you want, fly the planes upside down . . . just remember . . . we take care of each other. And we take care of customers. Within those bounds, you can do just about anything" (Gendron 1985, p. 28).

Freeing employees from workplace prisons that suppressed their humanity and creativity was a promising mission, but it was only part of what Burr wanted to do. He also wanted to establish employees as owners and managers. He envisioned "as far back as the dream-time days in Houston, . . . a company . . . organized to serve each employee individually by giving ownership, direct participation in its affairs, the freedom to fashion a personal contribution, and an opportunity for personal growth" (Rhodes 1984,p. 50). He contrasted his humanist quest with conventional ap- proaches: "Most organizations believe that humans are generally bad and you have to control them and watch them and make sure they work. At People Express, people are trusted to do a good job until they prove they definitely won't" (Whitestone and Schlesinger 1995, p. 4).

## A Decentralized Structure

Although decentralized, People Express centered control in a strategic apex consisting of Burr and six managing officers. Nine general managers formed the middle line. The operating core consisted of flight, maintenance, and customer service personnel. Managing officers provided leadership in thirteen functional areas (Whitestone and Schlesinger 1995, pp. 10–11). If an employee was asked to describe his or her job, the noun would be *manager* and the descriptive adjective would include *flight, maintenance,* or *customer service.* There were just those three People Express job categories. Pilots were flight managers; mechanics, maintenance managers; and reservationists, flight attendants, and baggage handlers, customer-service managers.

Each category was a horizontal differentiation of duties and functions rather than a vertical allocation of hierarchical authority.

### Mini-Airlines

The company's structural arrangements, however, were never set in stone. During the latter half of 1984 and into 1985, People Express continued to restructure. The problem was how to "re-create the small, close groups of the early days." With a workforce now numbering over 3,000 employees, the solution was to create operating groups of 250 to 300 employees. Each, like a "mini-airline," was responsible for its own aircraft, gates, routes, and cities (Holland and Beer 1993, p. 13).

Permeating the "mini-airlines" concept was a management philosophy that reflected Burr's first precept, commitment to the growth and development of people. Though some would argue that Burr looked at human nature through rose-colored glasses, he continued to believe employees could and should manage themselves. This meant aligning personal goals with organizational goals and encouraging people to monitor their own progress and even to take corrective action when their performance fell short (Holland and Beer 1993). A training director explained self-management: "We don't want to teach behaviors; we want to teach what the end result should look like and allow each individual to arrive at those results his or her own way" (Whitestone and Schlesinger 1995, p. 12).

Burr expected employees to echo his mantra of being "affirmative, up with people" (Holland and Beer 1993, p. 7). The litmus test for job applicants was not a typical formula from a personnel manual nor a rigorous analysis. As Burr explained, "Our main criteria was whether we'd want to go to dinner with them" (p. 7). Burr was convinced that applicants who failed to embrace the "wide openness" of the company as well as accept the chance to make a lot of money would not fit with People's precept-infused culture.

### Job Rotation

Maintaining structural flexibility required rotating employees from job to job. Burr believed this not only enhanced individual development but increased productivity. People Express' approach to rotating personnel initially required each employee to spend part of every month on the ground and part in the air. Ideally, the typical employee would fly 50 percent of the time and spend the other 50 percent on the ground alternating between aircraft servicing and staffing functions (Holland and Beer 1993). However, as time passed, employees began to show the strains.

Good theory became bad practice. Burr's obsession with growth placed more and more demands on the carrier's understaffed workforce. As a result, physical and emotional burnout took its toll. Brushing aside the fact that he was demanding more of people than they could deliver, Burr turned philosopher:

> Human beings are prepared and can operate at levels far in excess of what they think they can do. If you let them think they're tired and ought to go on vacation for two years or so, they will. . . . Now there are a lot of people who argue that you ought to slow down and take stock and that everything would be a whole lot nicer and easier and all that. I don't believe that. People get more fatigued and stressed when they don't have a lot to do. (pp. 21–22)

Ironically, a utopian strategy created a hellish environment, one that eventually erupted.

## A Southwest Wannabe

During the seven years Burr and Lorenzo worked together at Texas International, Burr kept an eye on Southwest Airlines. Southwest had evolved a people-friendly airline that was envied by the rest of the industry. In addition, the maverick airline had championed discount fares long before deregulation. Burr carefully observed Southwest's success and concluded that if Southwest could run a low-cost, people-centered airline in Texas, he could do the same in New Jersey.

Very often the first word in a company's name is important symbolically. "People" expressed Burr's vision of "develop[ing] a better way for people to work together" (Holland and Beer 1993, p. 4). According to Harvard professor D. Quinn Mills, People Express was a "comprehensive . . . effort to fit a business to the capabilities and attitudes of today's workforce" (Byrne 1985, p. 81).

If imitation is the highest form of flattery, Southwest should have felt a sense of pride as People Express took flight. At Texas International, Burr had "introduced 'Mr. Peanut' as the embodiment of . . . new, low-cost 'peanuts fares'" (Rhodes 1984, p. 44). He did this to increase the payloads on flights, and the deep discount policy continued at People Express. For example, USAir's fare from New York to its Pittsburgh hub was $123. On the same route, the People Express fare was $19. In each market, People Express undercut its competition. On average, passengers could save as much as 55 percent during peak hours and as much as 75 percent nights and weekends (Whitestone and Schlesinger 1995).

People Express offered no-frills flights. The carrier had no ticket counters; passengers were ticketed on the plane. The fare did not include having luggage checked or being served food, although for an extra fee, both services were available. Like Southwest, People Express counted on its spirited workforce to make flying fun. The message was simple: "At People Express attitude is as important as altitude" (p. 8).

To offer discounted fares, People Express had to monitor its costs per passenger-seat-mile, keep its planes in the air longer than other airlines, and make sure its employees were more productive than those at other companies. At one time, People Express' individual passenger costs were 5.2 cents per mile as compared to the industry's average of 9.4 cents. People Express planes flew an average of 10.36 hours per day, while competitor planes were in the air only 7.06 hours. Employees at People Express were approximately 1.5 times more productive than their counterparts. All of these factors contributed to the company's extraordinary 15.3 percent return on revenue, second only to Southwest.

Such phenomenal growth is unheard of in any business, much less an upstart airline. Burr was hailed as one of America's great entrepreneurs and appeared on the front covers of numerous business journals. One cover story quoted Burr as saying, "We have a unique problem. We've designed a product which is so popular we can't satisfy the demand" (Rhodes 1984, p. 42).

## Forgotten Precepts

People Express' initial route structure served the industry's back-country, shunned by the major carriers. But as these original roots became entangled in new growth, they began to deteriorate. Burr moved away from his niche as a regional discount airline and began competing with American, United, and Delta. Here he encountered the harsh reality of another law of economics: diminishing returns. He obviously had forgotten Southwest's first secret of success: "Stick to what you're good at."

### The First Weakness

Attempting to serve major metropolitan airports uncovered two of People Express' weaknesses. The company's computer technology was obsolete, and its operating infrastructure lacked trained personnel. Nevertheless, Burr plowed ahead. People Express entered the Chicago market, home of United. It then began service to Dallas, stronghold of American. If these two aggressive forays were not enough, it challenged Delta on its Atlanta turf. All three ventures magnified the limitations of the airline's antiquated computer reservations system. Rationalizing his devastating defeats at the hands of airline giants, Burr reflected, "They took our price advantage away. It was that simple" (Barrett 1991, p. 50). He was referring to the computerized yield management systems of the major carriers.

As mentioned earlier, yield management was perfected by American's Bob Crandall. It later became a major competitive weapon against discounters. Lacking a computer reservations system, People Express could monitor but one fare, which during off-peak hours was reduced even further. Through yield management systems, major carriers could match Burr's prices with enough reduced-fare seats to remain competitive. Thus yield management exposed People's weakness in the area of technology.

### The Second Weakness

The second major challenge to People Express' competitive edge was an overburdened infrastructure. A crucial element that was lacking was a balance between leadership and management. People Express was well led but poorly managed. Speaking to a group of employees in 1982, Burr continued to focus on setting new growth objectives and adding new aircraft, but he refused to acknowledge the continuing need to manage the airline. People's expansion was outpacing staffing needs, and its infrastructure was incapable of supporting rapid growth.

Burr's top executives tried to warn him. Gerald Gitner, one of the founders, on more than one occasion attempted to arouse Burr from the hypnotic humanist emphasis of the precepts. Gitner was a technical wizard and an astute manager. Even though Burr admired his abilities, the two simply did not view the company through the same lens. Burr focused on the big picture; Gitner monitored every detail. Gitner explained, "The guy [Burr] doesn't know details; he doesn't understand which of his routes are profitable or not" (Prokesch 1986, p. 8).

Gitner eventually left People Express and joined Pan Am. Burr tried to explain his departure: "He was much more oriented toward routes and planes and tell[ing] people what to do. . . . The competitive business strategy that I doped out, which relies on enabling the individual to do well, he just couldn't get comfortable with" (Rhodes 1984, p. 52). Gitner's take was different: "Participative management was supposed to be a means to an end: a profitable company. Burr forgot about the end. He thought management was his strong suit, but the results speak for themselves" (Prokesch 1986, p. 8).

## Effects of Poor Management

As People Express continued its meteoric growth, poor management took its toll on the airline's workforce. Pilots were asked to help schedulers determine flight crews or to substitute for dispatchers (Whitestone and Schlesinger 1995). Some questioned the validity of the precept-centered philosophy, prompting Burr to claim,

"Pilots have a character flaw. They have an innate sense of superiority and entitlement. Aggressive males are drawn to piloting. . . . It's heavily left-brain dominant, very well toilet trained" (Petzinger 1995, p. 116). The disdain was mutual. Pilots joked among themselves, asking each other, "Have you had your Kool-Aid today?" (p. 274). They equated Burr with Jim Jones, infamous founder of Jonestown, the social commune whose members en masse ended their lives by drinking a poison-laced concoction. By swallowing Burr's precepts, pilots were inferring, People Express employees were killing themselves. Long hours and inadequate training were gradually exacting a price.

Cross-training employees proved to be both a blessing and a curse. Rotation every month exposed employees to different functions and reduced boredom but undermined mastery of important technical skills. A team of student researchers referred to the cross-training policy as making People Express "a perpetually young company" (Booker et al. 1996). Constant emphasis on technical skills ran counter to Burr's humanistic intentions. Mental and physical burnout was common. As they moved from job to job, employees felt a lack of competence. Physically demanding hours caused enormous stress. Both employees and airplanes were pushed to their limits. Many employees began to think of the airline's headquarters as a second home. Divorces increased among employees, as did illness—and that included Burr (Whitestone and Schlesinger 1995). The health of the airline and its employees desperately needed attention.

The company's New Jersey terminal, designed to handle no more than 100,000 people a month, appeared to be a maze. Often, upwards of 1 million people struggled through the north terminal's narrow corridors. Boardings began to decline, the result of countless bumpings of passengers from overbooked flights. To reserve a seat on a People Express flight, customers had to go through an antiquated switchboard system. On some days, as many as 6,000 calls failed to get through the patchwork of part-time operators manning reservations desks (Petzinger 1995). People began to vote with their dollars. When Burr's mother called in November 1985 to inform him of her Thanksgiving travel to his brother's home, a dour note was struck: She had booked her flight on American Airlines ("Decline of People Express" 1988).

Reflecting on the downward spiral of People Express, Burr admitted failing to grasp the changes brought about by technology: "It went from a horse and buggy on January 18 to cars on January 19. It was like standing there with a revolver against a Gatling gun" ("Decline" 1988). In a sense, Burr became a prisoner of his own goal: growth, growth, and more growth. He explained his obsession, saying, "High growth is important to hotshot people. Our people want opportunity; without growth, they'd be gone. It's where you get your excitement and your learning; it makes for commitment and high levels of energy" (Glassman 1986, p. 11). He overlooked the obvious downside of too-rapid growth that demoralized both the company's employees and its customers.

Burr never heeded the wisdom of others who warned that his airline was out of control. The company was not the only thing out of control—so was its leader. Adulation from the national media drowned out the voices of reason. Burr did not listen to his managers or to his board. Even worse, he ignored the message of his own precepts.

Burr had built People Express "precept upon precept . . . line upon line" (Isaiah 28:10). But as the company guru he forgot precept five, simplicity, or sticking to your knitting. This means do not change your original market strategy, do not enter the land of the giants, and do not adopt another's religion until you cement the philosophical foundations of your own. Had Burr heeded his fifth precept, People Express might still be flying, delivering on his sixth precept: maximizing profits.

## Dancing with His Opposite

When Burr referred to a revolver versus a Gatling gun, he was comparing People's obsolete reservations system with American's yield management technology. In refusing to modernize People Express, Burr, in effect, was refusing to heed the voice of his more rational side, personified by Crandall. Burr's stormy relationship with Lorenzo reflects the same tendency to favor people over systems.

As a youngster watching planes take off, Burr imagined them flying over horizons to more just and humane worlds. He carried this vision throughout his airline career. Shortly after joining Lorenzo at Texas International, Burr proposed a new culture for the beleaguered airline, one that would bring more meaning to the lives of employees. These humanist leanings were thwarted by Lorenzo's politicist, and even rationalist, inclinations. As a result, Burr left and started his own airline.

But, just as he had done at Texas International, Burr failed to dance with his opposite, his rational side, at People Express. He refused to adopt the technology that would allow planes to transport people at competitive fares. He also overlooked the effects of his humanist principles on employees. His concern for humanity overshadowed a respect for rational analysis. The lack of balance eventually grounded his planes, bringing an end to his boyhood dreams.

It's interesting to note that *Star Wars* is Burr's favorite movie (Rimer 1984). Perhaps Burr imagines himself playing the leading role. The film pits Luke Skywalker's forces of light against Darth Vader's forces of darkness. Burr appears to identify with Skywalker, whose sole mission is the overthrow of Vader's evil empire. Adapted to People Express and the airline industry, *Star Wars* portrays the struggle between Donald Burr and the industry's Frank Lorenzo, a quest to liberate corporate workers from tyrannical managers.

# BETTY FRIEDAN:
# A HUMANIST IN THE WOMEN'S MOVEMENT

*"[W]herever I have gone since my childhood ... I have exulted in the sense of warm community, especially a community that appreciated and welcomed difference."*

(Friedan 2000, p. 29)

In many cultures, women play lesser roles in society's institutions than do men. But "the times, they are a-changing." For many

**FIG. 12**

## Betty Friedan: A Humanist in the Women's Movement

American women, things began to change in the 1960s when Betty Friedan's *The Feminine Mystique* was published. Her book became something of a women's manifesto. Friedan's purpose in writing the book was to expose society's perception "which defined woman solely in terms of her three-dimensional sexual relation to man as wife, mother, [and] homemaker" (Friedan 1964, p. 49). To her, the plight of women was "the problem that [had] no name" (Friedan 1963, p. 15), hence her choice of the word *mystique* in the book's title. Figure 12 presents Friedan's leadership profile.

In too many organizations, women find themselves trapped beneath glass ceilings. These invisible barriers confine women to professional levels below men. Women may feel their sense of self-worth at work constantly being attacked, making the barriers psychic, as well as economic, prisons. By championing women's rights, Friedan strikes a deeper nerve: a women's sense of self. *The Feminine Mystique* spurs women to view themselves as more than homemakers, as being able to play larger roles in society than those of wife and mother. These roles historically kept women from pursuing their own personhood. Friedan termed this new state of awareness "the fourth dimension" (1964, p. 47). Reaching it "required the emergence [of women] from passivity and biology and men's laws" (Friedan 2000, p. 201).

## A Young Humanist Emerges

"How tall I am!" Three-year-old Betty Friedan described herself while peering into her mother's bedroom mirror (2000, p. 15). Nearly eighty years later, Friedan reflects "What made me see myself as tall back then in Peoria?" Perhaps the image forecast the larger-than-life role she would later play in the lives of women. Her childhood nightly prayers support this view. Before going to sleep, Friedan prayed, "When I grow up, I want a work to do" (p. 15). Her school principal, as though hearing her prayers, challenged her: "You have a great talent for leadership. . . . You must use it for good, not evil" (p. 20). Years later, Friedan's best-selling *The Feminine Mystique* defined the work she wanted to do. Its pages reflect the passion of a woman to help other women find meaning beyond the home.

Friedan translated her principal's admonition to "do good" to righting the slightest injustice. Her father once observed during an argument that she possessed a "fine sense of justice." Friedan recalls "It was a question of dividing something—some fruit, oranges, bananas, or grapefruit?—and I objected loudly that the slices weren't equal. I don't think I was even the one getting gypped, but someone was" (p. 20). Eventually, that "someone" would multiply to women who were being shortchanged.

## Socialist Leanings?

When Friedan left home for Smith College, she resolved "to be the kind of woman for my husband and children my mother wasn't" (p. 31). She saw her mother as "never [having] anything that she thought was important to do" (p. 16). At Smith, Friedan edited the school paper, pursued her passion for psychology, and graduated summa cum laude. Through these activities, Friedan developed "a wonderfully clear, inescapable social conscience, an inescapable sense of political responsibility" (p. 55). As her social conscience developed so did her liberal leanings. This prompted her ascerbic father to wonder if he had sent his daughter to college "to be a communist" (p. 58). Friedan places her early idealism in its broader existential context:

> Using Freudian terms (and Jewish theology) to understand my original embrace of Marxism, I think, looking back, it gave first shape to my superego, my Jewish existential conscience, that sense which always seems to drive me, . . . that I have to use my life to make the world better, have to protest, step off that sidewalk and march against injustice. I wouldn't be the first Jewish thinker—in a long line of prophets and social theorists, up until now mostly male—to have applied that existential imperative, which may or may not stem from those tablets Moses brought down from the mountain or our personal experience of injustice as Jews, to the widest possible class of humanity of which we are part. (p. 71).

Summing up her undergraduate years, Friedan says, "Socialism had been the ideal in my left-wing youth" (p. 195).

## Leadership by the Pen

Throughout history, leaders have relied on various means to gather followers around a vision. Betty Friedan uses the pen. It was a questionnaire that gave birth to *The Feminine Mystique*. Two hundred of Friedan's fellow Smith graduates responded to probing questions about every area of their lives, including marriages, sex, children, and homes (Friedan 2000). Their combined answers helped Friedan frame "the problem that has no name." How to deal with this mystical female problem, "the crisis in [their] identity" (Friedan 1963, p. 69), became the focus of her book and, in turn, of the second wave of the women's movement.

When Friedan said she did not want to follow in her mother's footsteps, she meant that her horizons reached far beyond her family's front door. Her mother spent her adult life as a wife, mother, and homemaker. Her mother's life lacked what Friedan termed the "fourth dimension," or the fulfillment that comes from contributing to the world beyond the home (Friedan 1964). To establish themselves globally on an equal basis with men required women to overcome some powerful historical barriers. Such a breakthrough called for a drastic change: "women no longer being defined, defining themselves, solely in relation to men, as wives, mothers, sex objects, housewives, but defining themselves instead as people in society" (Friedan 2000, pp. 134–135).

As women read *The Feminine Mystique,* a common refrain emerged: "It changed my whole life" (p. 138). The book written to raise a woman's awareness about her plight in society began to elicit a large and loud chorus. Women were becoming aware of what they had been afraid to think, let alone say: "I want something more than my husband and my children and my home" (Friedan 1963, p. 32). They were ready to join forces.

## NOW

In June 1966, Friedan scribbled the opening line of the National Organization of Women's (NOW's) vision statement on a napkin: "to take the actions needed to bring women into the mainstream of American society now, exercising all the privileges and responsibilities thereof, in truly equal partnership with men" (Friedan 2000, p. 174). Later, in October, NOW was officially chartered. Friedan hailed the new coalition of women as "the second chapter of the American Revolution" (p. 180). NOW quickly became for women what the NAACP had been for African Americans. It gave women a voice—one with enormous power and influence—with which to participate in making their needs known.

### From Pen to Podium: A Change in Style

NOW forced Friedan into a more direct leadership role. Not only jobs, but training, control of their bodies, and childcare were important issues in the women's movement. Realizing the movement was more about equal rights than about gender, Friedan had to change hats. Giving diverse constituents with special interests some participative right in influencing Congress became imperative.

In the midst of her attempts to improve the welfare of women, Friedan had to wrestle with entrenched stereotypes. Women who embraced the movement were labeled "bra burners," "women's libbers," and "baby killers," among other epithets. Friedan was determined to keep the enterprise focused on "changing the conditions that made women rightfully angry, not getting stuck in a war of women against men" (Friedan 2000, p. 232). This forced her into a more hands-on approach.

After visiting with Prime Minister Indira Gandhi of India and studying her management-leadership style, Friedan drew some practical conclusions.

> Indira Gandhi was both feminine and authoritative in a style indubitably different from men's. I saw a woman dealing with the complexities of India, and sensed a style of thought and action that is different from win-or-lose, yes-or-no solutions. . . . I came to realize that women did not have to become like men or assume a male political style to be effective leaders. (pp. 193, 194–195)

Friedan never espoused a war of "women *versus* men, but [rather encouraged] women and men [to break] out of obsolete sex roles that prevented both . . . from being all [they] could be" (p. 190).

### The Airlines: NOW's First EEOC Test

NOW faced a daunting task of uprooting deeply entrenched sex biases in American society. Supposedly, the Civil Rights Act of 1964, particularly Titles VII and IX, had eliminated workplace sex discrimination. But the passage of legislation is one thing, and implementation is another. NOW's first sex discrimination challenge would be directed at the airline industry, and Friedan would lead the charge.

Airline policy included mandatory retirement of stewardesses when they married or reached their early thirties. "How could it not be sex discrimination to fire the stewardesses as soon as the first lines appeared around their eyes while allowing pilots to marry, have children, and age in the sky?" (Friedan 2000, p. 180). Forced to retire early, stewardesses would never establish enough tenure "to get good pay, good vacations, [or] good pensions. . . . It was in the airlines' best interest to fight the enforcement of Title VII, because women were a reliable source of cheap labor" (p. 181).

Following a prolonged court struggle, stewardesses prevailed. Years later, many stewardesses recognized Friedan on flights and offered champagne toasts to the woman who championed their need "to grow up and still fly" (p. 183).

### Choice?

Pro-life or pro-choice? No issue polarizes Americans more than abortion. An ongoing debate rages between pro-lifers and those who are pro-choice. Blood has been shed as abortion clinics have been bombed and doctors killed by fanatical opponents to what others consider legitimate women's rights.

Friedan refused to sidestep the issue of choice even though she herself "was never for abortion" (2000, p. 200). Taking a stand on an issue on which she was conflicted says much about Friedan's commitment. She fervently believed in a woman's right, and even need, to be responsible for her choice. If a woman was prohibited from making crucial decisions in one area of her life, she could be restricted in others. Friedan leaned on the U.S. Constitution to support her thinking: "For me the matter of choice has never been primarily the choice of abortion, but that you can choose to be a mother. That is as important as any right written in the Constitution" (p. 201). Without freedom in this sensitive area, women would not be granted free choices, not only at home, but also in jobs and education. Only a person placing the needs of others above her own would have taken so courageous a position.

## A "Two-Headed" Style

A two-headed woman appears on the cover of an issue of *Ladies' Home Journal* in which Friedan wrote an article in 1964. One head is a "Doris Day type housewife" and the other is "the emerging new career woman" (Friedan 2000, p. 157). This image symbolizes Betty Friedan's style. As "Doris Day," Friedan experienced the relational aspects of being mother, wife, and homemaker. As the new career woman, she experienced the rational aspects of working outside the home. Reflecting on her divorce, she said, "I could no longer be the two-headed woman I'd written about" (p. 224).

Friedan was committed to practicing what she preached. "How could I reconcile putting up with being knocked around by my husband while calling on women to rise up against their oppressors?" (p. 224). Friedan was doing what successful leaders do: building a trusting, personal bond with followers.

## Relationship: Roots of Leadership

Tirelessly and fearlessly, Friedan led women in their quest to secure equal rights. She spoke persuasively to millions of women, and her leadership reached well beyond *The Feminine Mystique*. Today, millions of women own their own businesses and the number is growing. Their presence in the executive suites of major corporations continues to expand. In the 1970s, women received roughly 4 percent of degrees awarded in law and medicine. Today they receive an estimated 40 percent (Friedan 2000, p. 376). If the past is prologue to the future, workplace advances on the part of females will continue to accelerate. Friedan's humanist vision for women has become a reality exceeding her original expectations.

At times, when opposition arose, whether inside or outside NOW, Friedan was forced into the role of manager. She researched issues with the dedication of one seeking a cure for a deadly disease. Then she fought critics with her findings, proving beyond doubt that women were treated as less than equal in most areas of society. But deep inside Betty Friedan was a leader whose vision for women's rights drove her, at times, to exhaustion. Many tried to paint her as a radical bent on changing existing social mores. But aren't most leaders radical agents of change?

Did Friedan disrupt the status quo? She did. But one must not overlook the integrity of her actions. Friedan's Old Testament heritage drove her to seek justice, even if it meant alienating friends and family. In a sense Friedan found herself in the role of a Moses. Whether or not she herself entered the promised land of women's rights, Friedan was determined to lead women there, and *The Feminine Mystique* served as her commandments.

Friedan explains her motivations to start a movement that has grown even beyond her wildest expectations:

> I did it for my father in a way, so that men would not have the burden of their wives' frustration at having to live through them. I did it for my mother, so that women would no longer have the discontent of dependency on their husbands, with no careers of their own. And I did it for my children, so that children would not have the burden of their mothers having to live through them. (p. 378)

## Dancing with Her Opposite

When Friedan thought of herself as two headed, one head symbolically was feminine, the other masculine. "Doris Day" symbolized her relational aspect of Eve, and the "career woman" symbolized her rational aspect of Adam.

The women's movement reflected Friedan's humanist leanings, but not at the expense of her rationalist, politicist, and culturist strengths. It would have been impossible to conceptualize the feminine mystique without a culturist's ability to envision the future, or to go to the exhaustive emotional limits she did without having the humanist's passion for others. Yet, Friedan was also able to dance with her opposites when the situation called for managerial savvy or political clout.

That "every institution in America was becoming aware" (Friedan 2000, p. 212) as a result of her efforts underscores Friedan's influence. Raising awareness is what leaders do. Friedan's dominant humanist side drove her to meet the needs of women beyond the home. Her culturist side allowed her to envision how meeting these needs would bring meaning to women's lives and self-awareness.

*The Feminine Mystique* reflects Friedan's struggle to embrace her opposite. It also reflects the struggle our male-dominated society has in reconciling opposing realities. Our society seems more rational than relational. Many men have forced their Eves into their unconscious in the same way society's unconscious drives have forced women into inferior roles. Thus, *The Feminine Mystique* is also a book for men, serving as a guide that alerts men to their suppressed feminine tendencies.

# JIMMY CARTER:
# A HUMANIST IN THE PRESIDENCY

*"The safety and well-being of the American hostages became
a constant concern for me, no matter what
other duties I was performing as President."*

(Carter 1982, p. 459)

A clergyman who viewed politics as less than honorable once asked Jimmy Carter why he was considering public service. Carter responded, "How would you like to be pastor of a church with 80,000 members?" (1975, p. 92). Carter's answer reveals two things: He cares about people, and his sense of what he could accomplish in the rough-and-tumble world of politics was naive.

With childlike faith, Carter believed he "could present a bill to Congress that seemed patently in the best interests of the country and the Congress would take it and pretty well pass it" (Barber 1992, p. 436). Carter's optimism stemmed from his puzzling ap-

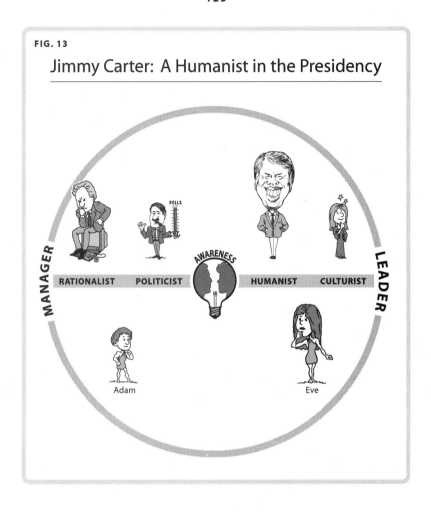

**FIG. 13**

## Jimmy Carter: A Humanist in the Presidency

proach to leadership. He cared about people but also about detail. No politician scrutinized pieces of legislation more closely. His engineering background portrays Carter as a rationalist. Yet, at a more basic level, his Christian faith contributes to his image as a humanist. On the surface, his rationalist leanings seemed to prevail. But in times of crisis, Carter retreated to his humanist roots. Figure 13 highlights his dominant feature but also shows his rationalist side.

Carter's "capacity to link large ideas to deep data bases" (p. 432) appeared as a strength. But, on more than one occasion, his obsession with detail forced him into an untenable position. Once he gathered enough facts to support his position, he refused to compromise with legislators. Carter did not believe they appreciated his attempt to use legislation as a humanist tool. One writer viewed Carter as "an information freak"; "homework was his stylistic strength . . . negotiation [his] stylistic weakness" (p. 444).

An inability to see the forest for the trees is the reason often given for Carter's lackluster presidency. Carter was widely perceived as a micromanager. But the roots of his leadership style reach beyond a rationalist's ability to deal with details, penetrating to the core of a humanist.

## Engineer's Mind, Humanist's Soul

Following graduation from Annapolis, Carter entered submarine training. Admiral Hyman Rickover, developer of the atomic submarine, supervised his apprenticeship. Rickover, notorious for hypercritical outbursts, was an extension of Carter's father, Earl. Carter was trained by his dad to get up an hour before daylight to work on the family peanut farm. The mental discipline required to manage a peanut farm was just as demanding as commanding a submarine. Rickover, like Earl, left no stone unturned.

> He always insisted that we know our jobs in the most minute detail, which is really a necessary basic characteristic of good submariners. He was often appalled at the incompetence of leaders who knew the theory of management but knew little about what actually occurred within their sphere of responsibility. (Carter 1975, p. 67)

Both mentors taught Carter a common lesson: Demand the best not only of yourself but of others as well. The title of Carter's autobiography, *Why Not the Best?*, echoes Rickover's challenge and his book *An Hour Before Daylight* underscores Earl's regimen.

Later in his life, Carter was forced to choose between the diverse paths Rickover and Earl exemplified. To the dismay of many, including his wife, Rosalynn ("Jimmy Carter" 1995), Carter forfeited a promising naval career to resume farming. But why did a man who appeared so rational let his heart overrule his head? Carter describes the choice:

> My most persistent impression as a farm boy was of the earth. There was a closeness, almost an immersion, in the sand, loam, and red clay that seemed natural and constant. The soil caressed my bare feet, and the dust was always boiling up from the dirt road that passed fifty feet from our front door. (2001, p. 15)

Even though Carter's head was pushing him toward a naval career, his heart was pulling him back to the farm.

## Political Beginnings

Carter's initial run for public office brought him face-to-face with politics' seamier side. Political potholes in the back roads of southwestern Georgia were treacherous. Losing a bid for the state senate by a slim margin, Carter discovered "the [ballot] box had been stuffed" (1975, p. 94). He challenged the results and, following an emotionally draining legal battle, won on a write-in ballot. Carter never forgot the experience.

> I really learned a lot from this first experience with politics. I began to realize how vulnerable our political system was to an accumulation of unchallenged power. Honest and courageous people could be quieted when they came to realize that outspoken opposition was fruitless. Those who were timid and insecure could be intimidated. . . . But there were other lessons I learned, too. The most vital was that people intimidated by corrupt public officials don't necessarily like it; if given some leadership and a chance, they are willing to stand up and be counted on the side of decency and of honest politics and government. (pp. 114–115)

Carter would later challenge Americans to stand up and be heard. With echoes of Watergate and Vietnam reverberating, he promised the nation he would reestablish integrity in a White House awash in scandal.

Hamilton Jordan's personal knowledge of Carter was exceeded only by that of family members (Mazlish and Diamond 1979). The longtime aide suggests a number of experiences that influenced Carter's determination to stand by the "small man."

> It's the rural South. . . . It's the influence of the church. It's growing up in the depression. . . . It's the military experience and engineering experience, and it's coming back to Plains and starting with nothing and being successful as a small businessman. It's exposure to politics. It's being a Democratic President, who's not performing as a Democratic President is supposed to. (pp. 13–14)

### Without Honor in His Own Country

"My name is Jimmy Carter and I'm running for president" ("Jimmy Carter" 1995). "Jimmy who?" was how most Americans responded as the unknown Georgian entered the 1976 presidential race. "Jimmy Carter" was not a household name, but the self-effacing peanut farmer was more formidable than he seemed. Behind the toothy smile was a man determined to prove that politics could be shaped to serve people's needs.

Referring to himself as "Jimmy" revealed Carter's down-home approach to politics. As one writer put it, "America would elect a new President called 'Jimmy' not only . . . by his intimates, but by every Tom, Dick, and Harry in the land" (Barber 1992, p. 398).

Carter never thought of himself as a member of the dominant social order of his hometown, saying, "During my childhood I never considered myself a part of the Plains society, but always thought of myself as a visitor when I entered that 'metropolitan' community" (1975, p. 22). Eventually, the nation began to see Carter as he saw himself: a visitor in Plains, a visitor in Georgia's governor's mansion, and a visitor in the White House.

## In the Arena: Debating Ford and Reagan

Carter promised the American people he would not lie to them and never did. However, his brutal honesty often got him into trouble. During his debates with Gerald Ford, Carter addressed an issue that he later admitted "could have cost me the campaign." Asked about his private life in a *Playboy* interview, Carter had confessed, "I've looked at a lot of women with lust. I've committed adultery in my heart many times. This is something God recognizes I will do—and I have done it—and God forgives me for it" ("Jimmy Carter" 1995).

Later in the Ford campaign, Carter returned to the *Playboy* interview, saying, "In retrospect . . . I would not have given that interview" ("Jimmy Carter" 1995). *Playboy,* he explained, was not the proper forum for discussing his strong Christian beliefs. Following defeat, Carter said his candor "was a devastating blow to our campaign." Yet his truthfulness says much about the man's integrity. Most politicians avoid speaking the truth. Carter spoke truthfully and paid a price.

If the Ford debates revealed Carter's heart, the Reagan debate made public his analytical skills. Carter pushed to have three or four debates. Reagan wanted only one. Carter's reasoning was "that I was much more a master of the subject matter and that he was a master of the medium." Carter believed that a number of debates would give him a chance to articulate issues in greater detail than his opponent. As a result he could undercut Reagan's showmanship. Carter approached the debates the same way he dealt with other areas of his presidency. Former speechwriter James Fallows offers an eyewitness account.

> Carter came into office determined to set a rational plan for his time, but soon showed in practice that he was still the detail man used to running his own warehouse, the perfectionist accustomed to thinking that to do a job right you must do it yourself. He would leave for a weekend at Camp David laden with thick briefing books, would pore over budget tables to check the arithmetic, and, during his first six months in office, would personally review all requests to use the White House tennis court. (1979, p. 38)

Whether Jimmy Carter was a great debater is questionable. But he was honest with himself and with the American people, a rare combination in today's "spin" politics.

## President or Chief of Staff

Quite possibly, a visitor to the White House might have thought Carter served as his own chief of staff (Barber 1992, p. 439). He was a "speed reader," "map scanner," "list-making blueprint planner," and "memorandum annotator," not to mention "tennis court scheduler" (p. 444). A fellow Democrat adds flesh to these bare-bones descriptions.

> [He] is an engineer without deep philosophic roots. . . .
> Carter is one of those super-achiever types you see in any
> high school—very intelligent, very ambitious. His whole life,
> its strong points and its weak points, revolves around this.
> He's a quick study. He's got a good mind. He absorbs information as quickly as anybody I've ever seen. But he's also an
> engineer who wants a comprehensive solution. (Johnson
> 1980, p. 295)

But Carter's penchant for details and order was offset by his humanist leanings. Here again James Fallows provides insight.

> Where Lyndon Johnson boasted of schools built and children fed, where Edward Kennedy holds out the promise of
> the energies he might mobilize and the ideas he might enact,
> Jimmy Carter tells us that he is a good man. . . . The central
> idea of the Carter Administration is Jimmy Carter himself,
> his own mixture of traits, since the only thing that finally
> gives coherence to the items of his creed is that he happens
> to believe them all. . . . No one could carry out the Carter
> program, because Carter has resisted providing the overall
> guidelines that might explain what his program is. . . .
> Carter thinks in lists, not arguments. (1979, pp. 34, 42)

Yet there is another side to Carter's style.

# A "Woman" President?

While in the White House, Carter the humanist often seemed to overrule his rationalist tendencies. Writer John Mihalec characterized his style as being more feminine than masculine.

> Jimmy Carter first presented himself to the nation as a masculine personality. Naval Academy. Submariner. Nuclear engineer. Farmer. Loner. Tough governor. But once in office, he lost no time revealing his true feminine spirit. He wouldn't twist arms. He didn't like to threaten or rebuke. He wore sweaters, and scrupulously avoided the trappings of power. He even kissed Brezhnev! And we watched how far this approach got him in the jungles of Washington and the world.
>
> So in a sense, we've already had a "woman" president: Jimmy Carter and his feminine style of leadership nearly drove us crazy. (1984, p. 30)

By many accounts, Carter's successes in office will be remembered as "nots." He did not dishonor himself, his office, or his country. He did not lead the country into war. He did not create blunders that precipitated crises at home or abroad. Given what went on before and after his presidency, these feats were significant in and of themselves (Johnson 1980). Having left office, Carter continues to demonstrate his humanist leanings.

## Hostages: A "Cancer" on the Presidency

"These last few days have been among the worst I've ever spent in the White House" are the words Carter used (1982, p. 459) to record the despair engulfing his presidency in February 1980. He describes the cause of his frustration: "The first week of November 1979 marked the beginning of the most difficult period of my life. The safety and well-being of the American hostages became a constant concern for me, no matter what other duties I was performing as President" (p. 459).

Ironically, what fueled Carter's moroseness was his compassion for the Shah of Iran. Against a wave of conflicting political and humanist opinions, Carter granted the Shah of Iran asylum while he underwent chemotherapy. Enraged by Carter's actions, a group of Iranian dissidents, supported by the Ayatollah Khomeini, seized the American Embassy, taking a number of Americans hostage. Carter's humanist feelings clouded his political judgment. After his emotions subsided, Carter realized he had ventured into a no-win political quagmire.

In his efforts to free the hostages, Carter fell back on his engineer's mind-set. His choices for action ranged "from delivering the Shah for trial as the revolutionaries demanded to dropping an atomic bomb on Tehran" (p. 459). After weighing his options, Carter settled on a meticulous plan. Disguised American soldiers aboard several helicopters would fly into the Iranian desert and proceed to the American embassy. Once there, they would storm and overpower the revolutionaries and free the hostages. The clandestine operation barely got off the ground. The plan involved synchronization of more parts than a nuclear submarine. American soldiers and helicopters were lost in the desert. Carter's presidency went into eclipse, and Ronald Reagan entered the White House.

Carter went without sleep the final three days of his presidency. He constantly monitored the hostage crisis. Dramatizing their disdain for Carter's compassion for the Shah, Iranian revolutionaries released the hostages thirty-three minutes after he left office. Carter 's response to the timing of the release was: "I guess one of the happiest moments of my life was after I had left office for 15 minutes and I was informed that the plane [carrying the hostages] had taken off. . . . That was a great moment" ("Jimmy Carter" 1995). Carter the humanist regarded the release of fifty-two Americans as being far more important than spending four more years in the White House.

## A Moslem, a Jew, and a Christian

In pursuit of Middle East peace, Carter invited Menachem Begin and Anwar Sadat to Camp David in September 1978. It was a high-water mark of his presidency, particularly its humanist dimensions. Following the agreement that was reached, one senator exhorted his colleagues to support Carter's candidacy for the Nobel Peace Prize (Barber 1992, p. 441).

The Camp David summit brought together leaders representing three of the world's great religions: Sadat was a Moslem, Begin a Jew, and Carter a Christian. When one considers the conflicting political interests, Carter's achievement is remarkable. But when one adds diverse religious forces, it becomes even more noteworthy. Carter's confidence that he could pull off the impossible began with his first meeting with Sadat in April 1977. Carter described this encounter as a numinous experience, "a shining light burst[ing] on the Middle East scene" (Carter 1975, p. 282).

Because of the acute differences separating the Israeli and Egyptian leaders, Carter believed he had to be involved in the summit's every detail. Many of the finer points in the agreement's twenty-three revisions were penned in his handwriting (Barber 1992, p. 442). Carter assumed his customary twin roles in the negotiations. He wore the hat of a humanist in convincing Sadat and Begin to cooperate, and he donned the analytical hat of an engineer in hammering out the details.

## From President to World Leader

"I have always looked on the presidency of the United States with reverence and awe, and I still do. But recently I have begun to realize that the president is just a human being" (Carter 1975, p. 177). Jimmy Carter entered the White House concerned about human beings and left with the same humanist inclinations. The Carter Center in Atlanta serves as the hub for Carter's "unfinished presidency" (Brinkley 1998). "What we're doing at the Carter Center is an extension of what we were doing in the White House" (p. 478). One writer observes Carter is the first president in history to leave the presidency for higher office, that of "Leader of the Whole Free World" (Barber 1992, p. 443).

In 2002 Jimmy Carter was awarded the Nobel Peace Prize in recognition of his humanitarian efforts throughout the world.

Asked if the honor would change his life, Carter responded, "It didn't change my life when I became a state senator, or governor, or president, or defeated candidate for re-election, and I don't think this will change my life, either. My roots are too deep here to be changed, and I'm too old" (Zoroya 2002, p. D4).

Carter's selection came as no surprise to many of his political colleagues. Former Georgia senator Sam Nunn added insight to the Nobel committee's decision: "He [Carter] has proved that world leadership depends as much on values you hold as the office you hold" ("Voice for Peace" 2002, p. A10). Another Georgian, Andrew Young, frustrated that Carter had not been awarded the prize earlier, said, "He's earned [it] at least three times before now" (p. A1). Both men agree that Carter practiced what he preached before he entered the White House, while he was there, and since he left it.

Though proud of his many accomplishments in the rough-and-tumble world of politics, Carter points to the years following his stay in the White House as being the most satisfying (Basu 2002, p. A11). Through the Carter Center (begun in 1984 and completed in 1986) Carter and his wife, Rosalynn, have traveled around the world helping the underprivileged. Their efforts prompted Andrew Young to conclude, "[They] live as disciplined, meaningful and purposeful lives as I've ever known, and they draw a certain unchallengeable moral power and joy from the process. In them truly, the meek have inhertited the Earth" (Young 2002, p. H8).

## Dancing with His Opposite

Viewing Carter's life across the years, one sees both humanist and rationalist leanings. Yet when push came to shove, as it did when his father, Earl, died, Carter emphasized his humanist convictions. He went back home to the farm where, as a boy, "the soil [had] caressed [his] bare feet." Mother Earth had a stronger pull on Carter than a naval career. Yet he proved he could dance with his rational side by graduating from the Naval Academy and training as a nuclear engineer under Rickover, the toughest of rationalists.

In addition, Carter's concern for the Shah of Iran, for the American hostages, and for peace in the Middle East reflects the fact that people came before the presidency. That one writer called him the leader of the free world and another saw him as a "woman" president only reinforces the assessment that Carter was as comfortable with his Eve as with his Adam.

Regardless of whether you see Carter as rationalist or humanist, his Achilles' heel is his political naïveté. Raised as a Baptist, he was accused of being too soft in the jungle of politics. Trained as an engineer, he was accused of micromanaging the presidency. Carter comfortably embraces his rational opposite. Yet his love for Mother Earth, for the Christian faith, and for the Carter Center's humanitarian efforts often undermined his political judgment.

## THREE PROFILES, ONE STYLE

The profiles of three leaders illustrate a humanist approach to running organizations. Does the way Burr, Friedan, or Carter handled situations remind you of yourself? Again, remember to focus on their styles, not their personalities.

- Do you consider personal values and human needs when making a decision, as opposed to facts and details?
- Are people more important to you than end results?
- Do you believe organizations and people can satisfy each other's needs?

If you answer yes, then you may find yourself positioned similarly to our three humanists.

### Burr

Burr's caricature reflects his humanist desire to meet the needs of People Express employees. Needs, participation, and people are pivotal to humanists. They tend to be dominated by their feminine Eve. Burr's Eve is depicted as larger than his Adam. Burr's style is far more humanist and culturist than rationalist and politicist. The name chosen for his airline, People Express, underscores his humanist leanings.

Burr failed because he refused to recognize his analytical weakness, the strength of Lorenzo and Crandall. Lorenzo forced Burr from Texas International and Crandall forced him from the industry. If Burr and Lorenzo had embraced each other, could they have dominated the industry? Had Burr adopted Crandall's technological innovations, would People Express still be flying?

## Friedan

Looking at Friedan's caricature, you find her on the right side of the continuum, dominated by her humanist leanings. But, unlike Burr, she was able to move to the left and embrace her rationalist and politicist sides.

*The Feminine Mystique* underscores not only Friedan's humanist concern for women but also her culturist vision for their escape from the home, a woman's psychic prison. As NOW built coalitions and established its power base, Friedan functioned as a politicist fighting the establishment through every legal channel possible. As NOW grew and factions within and without the women's movement developed, Friedan exercised her rational muscle. As a rationalist, she took a more authoritative, hands-on approach in order to hold NOW together.

But, as the women's movement evolved, Friedan's humanist passion began to parallel Lincoln's. Just as Lincoln refused to back down from his stance of freeing slaves, Friedan refused to back down from her position that women must be freed from the "mystique" by which society enslaved them.

## Carter

Like Friedan's, Carter's caricature stands on the right of the continuum. As Carter's profile demonstrates, neither his humanist nor his rationalist inclinations can be denied. The relative sizes of his Eve and Adam appear to support this conclusion. For a number of reasons, we believe Carter is more at home as a humanist than a rationalist.

When Carter returned home from what would likely have been a brilliant career in the navy, he was embracing his humanist roots, leaving the rational world of nuclear submarines behind. He might have become an admiral in the navy and managed thousands of sailors. Yet from his humble roots in Georgia he became president, believing he could use politics to better the lives of Americans. Unfortunately, humanist and rationalist impulses often eclipsed his political judgment.

Like Friedan, Carter was more than a humanist. He was often able to shift his approach depending on the circumstances. His observation that "the President is just a human being" shows his respect for being human. Carter is a humanist at heart.

Burr, Friedan, and Carter are effective individuals whose styles reflect humanist inclinations. If you did not identify with them, you can try on the culturist in the next chapter. Remember that even if you find yourself feeling more comfortable with the next three portraits, aspects of the rationalist, politicist, and humanist are still part of who you are.

# The Culturist

**symbolic**
## Culturist
**Intuition**

Culturists are symbolic leaders. They communicate through stories, rituals, and ceremonies rather than rational facts and figures. But this passion is not just for show. Symbolic leaders are hell-bent on shaping a culture in which higher calling and shared purpose capture people's hearts. Rather than govern by fiat and command, culturists rely on intangible, unobtrusive influence. This includes history, which holds vital lessons; shared values articulating what the enterprise stands for; heroes and heroines, living logos with words and deeds supporting deep-seated cultural commitments; ritual and ceremony drawing people together under a sacred canopy; and stories conveying widely held values and beliefs.

Stories are the culturist's stock-in-trade. Each story, whether it links the organization to the past, extols the present, or envisions the future, conveys a primary theme: "This is the way we do things around here." By telling stories, the culturist encourages people to buy into big-picture thinking. Success leads to an integrated organization in which people feel they are a part of something bigger than themselves, something that brings meaning to their lives at work.

Yet culturists often stumble over rational and political dimensions. At times, they become so captivated by their visions that they neglect to gather facts and build coalitions needed to support their visions. People simply cannot take the big leaps required by wholesale cultural changes as readily as they can make step-by-step changes espoused by rationalists and politicists.

How do culturists build meaningful environments? Profiles of three highly successful symbolic leaders follow. They are former Southwest Airlines CEO Herb Kelleher, entertainment celebrity Oprah Winfrey, and former president Ronald Reagan. Although their behavior encompasses the roles of rationalist, politicist, and humanist, all of these people are most comfortable in the role of culturist.

# HERB KELLEHER:
# A CULTURIST IN BUSINESS

*"I think the essence of it is making people feel as if they are real participants....To us there is no formula. It is not algebra, it is not a science, it's an art."*

(Turner and Newsom 1994, p. 46)

In 1966 Southwest Airlines launched a campaign seeking its fifth consecutive Department of Transportation "Triple Crown Award," which recognizes on-time performance, efficient baggage handling, and customer satisfaction. The theme of the campaign was "Gimme Five" (1996). Employees signed on, convinced that a fifth Triple Crown was a "gimme." As with their four previous awards, they would look back and boast, "We came, we saw, we kicked tail" (Gross 1993, p. 180). Herb Kelleher, Southwest's colorful CEO, promised to commemorate a fifth victory by having names of the

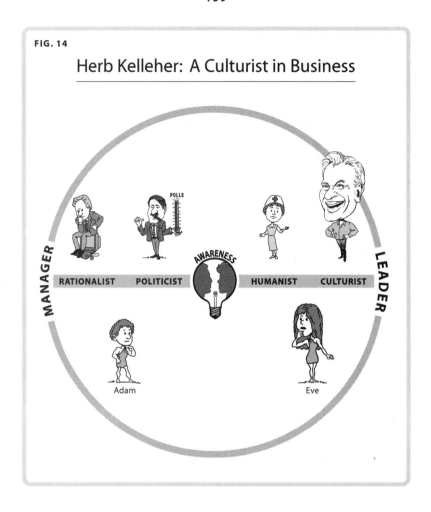

**FIG. 14**

## Herb Kelleher: A Culturist in Business

company's 25,000 employees imprinted on baggage bins of a new Boeing 737. As expected, Southwest won easily. Today that aircraft flies as a tribute to the airline's gutsy spirit.

Because Southwest excels in every area of its operations, it should come as no surprise that it maintains its top-ten position among America's most admired companies year after year. In 2002 and 2003 it was number two on the list (Stein 2003, p. 84). Herb Kelleher's symbolic leadership is the driving force behind the plucky airline's lofty rankings. Note his leadership position in Figure 14.

## From Slip-Up to Start-Up

"I always assumed I was a slip-up," Herb Kelleher self-effacingly reflects on his life (Jarboe 1989, p. 140). Some thirty-five years after his "slip-up birth," Kelleher and his close friend Rollin King founded Southwest Airlines. Before the new company got off the ground, Kelleher had to win a court battle. Competitors attempted to block Southwest from taking off. The early struggle became entwined in the company's lore and helped pave the way for the evolution of an unusual human institution.

Southwest had a humble beginning. In 1966 Kelleher and King scratched a triangle on a cocktail napkin depicting air travel connecting Dallas, Houston, and San Antonio. The napkin became a business blueprint ("Tale of Two Men" 1996). King, the owner of a struggling commuter operation, met with lawyer Kelleher under the pretense of discussing the dissolution of his company. But he really wanted to sell him on the idea for a new airline. King was convinced that the success of an intrastate airline lay in routes connecting larger metropolitan areas. As he explained,

> You got to have a commercially booming state with some really big cities far enough apart to make bus or car travel inconvenient. Offhand, I can't think of but two states like that. California's one—and that's why Pacific Southwest Airlines and Air California are going great guns as intrastate carriers. The other state is Texas, Herb, and we don't have an airline like that. (p. 3)

Kelleher responded with an enthusiastic, "Rollin, you're crazy. Let's do it!" (p. 3).

Southwest's silver anniversary publication ("Tale of Two Men" 1996) pictures Orville and Wilbur Wright sitting beside Herb Kelleher and Rollin King. The Wright brothers proved people could fly; Kelleher and King proved they could fly cheaply and have fun.

# A Pointed Philosophy

Southwest's route structure challenged the hub-and-spoke systems of airline giants such as American, Delta, and United. A system of city pairs allowed passengers to choose a direct route from city of origin to destination. King and Kelleher's point-to-point philosophy established a low-fare, bare-bones niche in the airline industry and an attractive draw for potential customers.

The company received its corporate charter on March 15, 1967. Some eight months later, Kelleher filed with the Texas Aeronautics Commission (TAC) for the right to provide service between Dallas, Houston, and San Antonio. About a year after Air Southwest incorporated, the state commission granted the company its certificate (Jarboe 1989). Immediately, Air Southwest's certification was blocked by Braniff and Texas International. The two airlines argued that they already served the three metropolitan areas. On August 6, 1968, a district court agreed.

The legal battle moved to the appellate court, which upheld the lower court's decision. This setback caused Southwest's investors to lose heart. Kelleher bolstered their sagging morale by offering to work free and to shoulder all legal costs himself. His offer paid off: in 1970, the Texas Supreme Court overruled the appellate court. The dispute then moved to the Civil Aeronautics Board (CAB), which dismissed the complaint. Lawyers for Braniff and Texas International sought a restraining order from a state judge. Their petition succeeded. Less than forty-eight hours before inaugural takeoff, Southwest was again grounded ("Tale of Two Men" 1996).

Kelleher was not to be stopped. He persuaded a Southwest pilot to fly him to Austin aboard one of the airline's Boeing 737s. At the state capital, he headed for the supreme court building. Tom Reavley, one of the supportive justices in the court's 1970 opinion, urged fellow justices to attend a special morning session of the court. There, Kelleher would be allowed to argue Southwest's case (Petzinger 1995). In preparation, Kelleher worked the entire night. He petitioned justices to set aside the lower court's restraining order. Again, the state's highest tribunal ruled in favor of Southwest. Kelleher called Southwest's president, Lamar Muse, to inform him of the victory. "That's great, Herb," Muse responded, "But what the h— am I gonna do when that sheriff shows up tomorrow morning at seven, telling me we can't take off?" Kelleher fired back, "Lamar, you roll right over him! Leave our tire tracks on his uniform if necessary" ("Tale of Two Men" 1996).

On schedule the next day, June 18, 1971, Southwest's planes took off. But more turbulence lay ahead. Southwest was soon back in court to argue for its right to fly from Love Field. After another march through state and federal courts, the company again prevailed (Petzinger 1995).

If adversity breeds character, Southwest's idiosyncratic character was formed early on. As Kelleher observes, "That period has been very helpful to Southwest Airlines ever since. Our people learned that they had to be warriors, that there was a lot of risk in life, that the existence of Southwest was in jeopardy on a day-to-day basis. It's a valuable legacy" (Tenney and Smith 1990, p. 50).

## Cars in the Skies

To succeed in its special niche, Southwest had to go head-to-head with the automobile. Kelleher described this "grounded" competitor: "We're competing with the automobile, not the airlines. We're pricing ourselves against Ford, Chrysler, GM, Toyota, and Nissan. The traffic is already there, but it's on the ground. We take it off the highway and put it in the airplane" (Chakravarty 1991, p. 49). To meet this challenge, Kelleher recognized Southwest's competitive edge: fares, frequency, and fun.

### Fares

In a drastic move to increase loads, Southwest began offering $10 one-way after-hours fares between Houston and Dallas. The strategy paid off. Within weeks, the flights were completely booked. Southwest then began offering two fares: a peak-hour rate of $26 and an off-peak rate (nights and weekends) of $13. This two-tier pricing system was a marketing tactic that would revolutionize the industry's rate structure ("Tale of Two Men" 1996).

Braniff countered by offering a $13 fare on Southwest's only profitable route: Dallas to Houston. Southwest retaliated by offering its passengers a choice: pay the normal $26 fare and receive a fifth of Chivas Regal, Crown Royal, or Smirnoff or purchase Braniff's $13 ticket. Opting for the $26 fare got passengers a free bottle of liquor, and business travelers could turn in an expense voucher for the full fare. Beating Braniff at its own game, Southwest became the state's largest distributor of premium liquors.

Years later, Southwest went to the mat with America West. The Phoenix-based carrier ran a series of ads showing Southwest travelers wearing sunglasses or covering their heads to hide the fact that they were flying on an "unsophisticated" airline. Kelleher entered the battle disguised as the "unknown flier." He appeared in ads with a paper bag over his head. As he removed the bag, dollars spilled out. Peering over the bag, Kelleher issued a challenge: "If you're embarrassed to fly the airline with the lowest customer complaints in the country, Southwest will give you this bag" (Petzinger 1995, p. 289).

## Frequency

The frequency component of Southwest's short-haul philosophy depends on a finely tuned system of competition between labor and management. The airline's celebrated ten-minute turnaround time between flights was the outgrowth of a ruling prohibiting its out-of-state charter service. In 1972, the carrier had purchased a fourth aircraft to supplement its regular service. Complying with the judge's prohibition, Southwest then sold the airplane. But how could Southwest maintain regular service without the fourth aircraft? An employee came up with the solution: By shortening gate time, three planes could be in the air longer. With a ten-minute turnaround, in fact, the three planes could provide the service of four. Today the ten minutes has increased to twenty. But Southwest still boasts the industry's fastest turnaround time by twenty-five minutes ("Tale of Two Men" 1996). When asked why Southwest was able to turn its planes around so quickly, Kelleher quipped, "One of our real smart guys at Southwest Airlines who almost graduated from high school told me that basically people are willing to pay you for flying, not sitting" (Kelleher 1997).

To maintain high frequency, Southwest utilizes only Boeing 737 jets. Early on, Kelleher concluded that using one type of aircraft creates tremendous economies of scale. The 737s are more fuel efficient than other aircraft, reducing a major cost. Because the fleet's parts are basically the same, they can be obtained more cheaply. Moreover, a unified parts system allows maintenance crews to be trained more efficiently, and flight training is less costly if pilots are certified to fly one type of aircraft.

### Fun

Then there is the matter of fun. On a shoestring budget, Southwest received a lion's share of positive publicity. Early on, Kelleher and his associates determined that "Southwest Airlines wanted to be known as a fun, absolutely outrageous company" ("Tale of Two Men" 1996).

The spirit that permeates Southwest is spelled in many ways: "L-U-V," "F-A-M-I-L-Y," and "V-A-L-U-E-S." But the word that makes working at Southwest special is F-U-N. Walk the halls at Southwest's headquarters, purchase a ticket at its ticket counters, wait in a boarding area, or move about the cabin during flight. You will be engulfed by the spirit of play. This fun attitude is reflected in a colorful rap shuffle, "Just Plane Fun." As the lead rapper, Kelleher delivers two stanzas:

> Southwest shuffle is the tendency to move,
> When you're feeling good, when you're in the groove;
> From break of day to setting sun,
> At Southwest Airlines, we have fun.
>
> My name is Herb, big "Daddi-O,"
> You all know me—I run the show;
> But without your help, there'd be no Luv,

On the ground below or in the air above;
You're truly my source of strength and pride,
And I sure am glad you're on my side.
("Just Plane Fun Shuffle" n.d.)

Fun for Southwest employees and passengers begins on the ground and continues in the air. This genuinely playful spirit is breathed into the enterprise by Kelleher, who says, "We take our competitors seriously, but not ourselves" ("Tale of Two Men" 1996).

## A Family Affair

Unlike its competition, Southwest has never experienced a debilitating strike. This is a tribute to Kelleher's leadership in fostering the airline industry's first employee profit-sharing plan. To show appreciation, a combined group of pilots from Southwest and Morris (the Utah-based airline acquired by Southwest) presented Kelleher with his favorite toy: a custom-made Harley-Davidson motorcycle.

Pilots are not the only employees who appreciate Kelleher's leadership. So, too, do flight attendants and others. Kelleher explains his leadership style:

You have to follow somebody else's lead. In that way you show you are a good leader, because you are not letting your ego stand in the way of doing what's right for the company. To follow the right path, you have to be willing to listen to other people, to accept their judgments when they are superior to yours, and to follow them. ("Herb Kelleher Speaks on Leadership" n.d.)

Even when he has to lay aside his own ego, Kelleher heeds this philosophy. In negotiations with the flight attendants' union, Kelleher was asked, "What blockhead put this policy into effect?" Sheepishly, Kelleher owned up, "I'm the blockhead to whom you refer."

## Of People and Culture

In 1983, Southwest breathed life into its fairy-tale image by naming its pudgy mascot airplane, T. J. LUV. The mascot came to symbolize the underlying myth about Southwest's culture. "Myth is neither true nor false, but behind truth—as that body of material through which a culture's values, purpose, and direction come to expression" (Owen 1987, p. 10). Symbolically the little airplane, ever true to itself, expresses the values that weave their way through Southwest's ways. These are reflected in rituals and celebrations speaking to the hearts of all the company's employees.

Calvin Coolidge once said, "The business of business is business." Kelleher rejoins, "The business of any business is people, people, people"("Herb Kelleher Speaks on Leadership" n.d.). To further emphasize his point, Kelleher tells the story of a young friend who recently bought a business. Meeting the man's wife, Kelleher asked, "How's the business going?" She complained that her husband was spending 90 percent of his time dealing with people. Kelleher retorted, "That is a smooth-running organization. I spend 99.8 percent of my time on people issues" ("Herb Kelleher Speaks on Leadership" n.d.).

When a group of people speaks the same language, shares common values and beliefs, and practices familiar behaviors, they are members of a shared culture. Southwest extols its people and their culture. A stroll through the corridors of corporate headquarters is a walk through a gallery of employees and their families. On a Southwest plane, you could be flying on a whale *Shamu* or a valentine with a heart prominently emblazoned on the fuselage. Attending celebrations at Southwest is like moving from one party to another, experiencing many different forms of entertainment. Encountering the Southwest culture, in the air or on the ground, is like being invited into a special club. A young instructor at Southwest's University for People observed, "It's like going to heaven without having to die."

Kelleher articulates the philosophy behind Southwest's vibrant spirit: "I've always thought—and this sounds simplistic and childish—that you can be a successful business and enjoy yourself at the same time" (Butler 1993, p. 52). Backing his puckish words with playful deeds, Kelleher appeared as Elvis Presley on a Harley-Davidson, as a leprechaun on St. Patrick's Day, as a rock singer at company events, and as a regular employee on Southwest flights. During his stint as a flight attendant, he helped serve "love potions" and "love snacks" to passengers. His culturist leadership contributed to Southwest's being ranked in the top ten of *The 100 Best Companies to Work for in America* in 1993. The company received a five-star rating for its camaraderie and friendliness (Levering and Moskowitz 1993).

Southwest's distinctive environment has become a standard for others to emulate. "They may be able to copy the strategy, but they will never be able to copy the culture," Kelleher once remarked, referring to competitors who flatter Southwest by attempting to copy aspects of its way of doing things. Earlier, Kelleher addressed the never-ending search for the latest management fad:

> We don't use any of those buzzwords around Southwest Airlines. . . . I think you find that the language, the formulated approach, pretty soon begins to confine you and cabin you. So we don't use Total Quality Management or any of those things, even though we may follow some of the precepts that are advanced. . . . I think the essence of it is making people feel as if they are real participants. . . . To us there is no formula. It's not algebra; it's not a science; it's an art. We give leadership training at Southwest Airlines—forget administering; forget management; what we want are leaders. That's the hardest thing to come by. (Turner and Newsom 1994, pp. 46, 48)

Colleen Barrett, Kelleher's longtime associate and now president of Southwest, echoed these sentiments as she explained the difficulties of conveying Southwest's mystique to other managers:

> I think they were waiting for me to give them a list: They wanted me to give them a twelve-point program, or to tell them the seven things they need to do to accomplish what

we've accomplished. I've often thought that maybe we should just make up a list and read it to them. It wouldn't be the way we did things, but I think they would go away a lot happier. . . . The great secret is that there is no secret. ("Getting High on Love and Laughter" 1995, pp. 61, 62)

Ed Stewart, Southwest's director of public relations, summarizes: "Culture at Southwest is the Golden Rule applied, not talked" (Stewart 1996).

### University for People
Southwest's University for People is committed to "developing leaders who make a difference." The training center offers an array of courses highlighting themes such as spirit and culture, experiential learning, POS (Positively Outrageous Service), humor, and team building. The emphasis is on soft skills as opposed to technical training. Teamwork, leadership, and communication are staples of the curriculum. Those who enroll are selected from an enormous pool of applicants.

In 1995, the airline received 124,000 applications; it interviewed 38,000 and hired 5,473 (Southwest Airlines 1995). Southwest selects people mainly because of their attitudes. A humorless person would be like a fish out of water, since humor is a key requisite for employment. One ad, in which Kelleher is portrayed as Elvis, reads, "Work for the airline where Elvis has been spotted" (Culture Day 1996). Then there is the story about a team of Southwest recruiters attempting to get a group of applicants to relax. They dropped their pants, displaying their SWA boxer shorts adorned with colorful red hearts. "Southwest," in the words of Kelleher, "is looking for other-oriented people, not people who study their own navels, no matter how pretty and lint free they might be. No one is the center of the universe" ("Herb Kelleher Speaks on Leadership" n.d.).

## Not a Typical Corporate Directory

The idea of not taking oneself too seriously is a central theme in Southwest's corporate directory, *Our Colorful Leaders* (1996). T. J.

LUV, Southwest's airplane mascot, is positioned on the front cover, crayoned with multiple colors extending haphazardly beyond the plane's outline. Below are the words "Southwest employees color outside the lines . . . and there's no better example than our leaders." Inside the directory, pictures of corporate officers are connected by crayons. Each executive is pictured twice: a passport photograph contrasted with a gag picture. Kelleher's images appear in the middle. In his gag picture, Kelleher appears in a lavender dress with a purple stole. His accessories include a pearl necklace, elbow-length gloves, and a flowered bonnet. An accompanying caption says, "Began coloring at Southwest in 1966."

Readers are encouraged to complete an outline of T. J. LUV on the back cover by connecting the dots numbered 1 to 58 and to color the plane's interior parts—outside the lines, of course. Instructions are clear:

> At Southwest Airlines, we're fortunate to work at a place where we are all encouraged to be leaders and to "color outside the lines." Our leaders give us the colors, paper, and sketch of our jobs. It is up to us to provide the imagination, ingenuity, and hard work to complete the drawing. (*Our Colorful Leaders* 1996).

Individual creativity is a corporate trademark. "Southwest has always been a very innovative company," Kelleher remarked to a group of company employees. He defined innovation as "doing things differently from the way they've been done before." He cited an example: the firm's use of cash register ticketing. Shortly after the introduction of these tickets, customers complained that they lost tickets. The tickets didn't look like tickets. Southwest considered changing the ticket's form, but an employee came up with the idea of writing on the ticket, "This Is a Ticket."

The inventive employee prevailed, but not without further incident. Kelleher illustrated the new problem with a story. A passenger, after purchasing his ticket, walked to his flight. On the way, he noticed his ticket did not state his destination. Bewildered, he returned to the ticket counter. "Lady, this doesn't say where I'm going." She responded, "Sir, don't you know where you're going?" (Kelleher 1997).

## Of Symbols, Celebrations, and Rituals

Southwest's spirit rests on a belief that if employees are respected, they will respect customers. The spirit is sung and "shuffled" at special corporate events; it is represented by paintings on aircraft like *Shamu One* and *Lone Star One;* it is reflected in acronyms like LUV (Southwest's NYSE ticker symbol), WIT (Whatever It Takes), POS (Positively Outrageous Service), and FFF (Fares, Frequency, and Fun); it is seen on special occasions, like Halloween and Valentine's Day, when employees dress in costumes to celebrate.

Southwest goes to great lengths to make sure employees are honored for outstanding performance. The "Heroes of the Heart Award" is a tribute paid to the members of Southwest's behind-the-scenes workers. This award was created by Southwest's Culture Committee. Its inaugural recipients were administrative coordinators, who manage behind-the-scenes operations. In typical Kelleher style, the lavish ceremony was held in a Love Field airport hangar. Decorations included hundreds of heart-shaped balloons. Several speakers defined a hero of the heart as any employee who recognizes that "attitude, altruism, dedication, and submergence of self to cause are as necessary as knowledge and expertise to achieving economic security" ("Heroes of the Heart" n.d.). In perfect harmony with the occasion, Kelleher presented their award: a new Boeing 737 aircraft with the inscribed words *Heroes of the Heart* and *Station Coordinators* prominently displayed.

No other incident better demonstrates Kelleher's symbolic awareness than a Dallas sports arena event. Inadvertently, Southwest purloined an aircraft service company's slogan, "Just Plane Smart," in a nationwide ad campaign. Realizing his potential legal liability, Kelleher responded favorably to Stevens Aviation CEO Kurt Herwald's suggestion that the two arm wrestle for the right to use the slogan. After agreeing to the event, the "combatants" began training. Herwald, a bodybuilder, trained with heavy weights in his local gym. Kelleher, a man given to drink and nicotine, did arm curls with bottles of Wild Turkey and increased his cigarette intake from two packs a day to five. The widely publicized event took place on schedule. In a two-out-of-three contest, Kelleher lost, proving that "lifting two bottles of Wild Turkey for a week is not the type of training of which arm wrestlers speak." Although he lost, Kelleher still won. Both firms received tremendous television and newspaper coverage at no cost. The issue was resolved and Southwest's cultural commitment to fun was reinforced ("Malice in Dallas" n.d.).

Symbols and celebrations are not the only soul languages spoken at Southwest. Rituals, too, are highly esteemed. Southwest's acquisition of Morris Airlines is a case in point. When Southwest acquired the regional carrier, the company went to great lengths to assure Morris employees they were joining a new family: The two airlines were wed in a Las Vegas ceremony. The Southwest groom wore a tuxedo with T. J. LUV attached to his cummerbund. The bride wore a white wedding gown with a Morris mascot airplane around her waist. "Elvis" performed the ceremony. The union was symbolized by placing a huge diamond ring over the neck of the Morris mascot. After the ceremony, the two mascots kissed, and the newlyweds cut the wedding cake decorated with the message Southwest Spirit Weds Morris Magic. Attendees drank a toast to the spirit and magic of the union as they sang, "We are family, Southwest Airlines, Morris, and me" ("Morris Airlines Wedding" n.d.).

When Southwest celebrated its silver anniversary in 1966, all employees were invited to the "deck party of the century" held at the company's Love Field headquarters. Six thousand attended. Those who couldn't make the Dallas party held their own local festivities. To commemorate the occasion, Southwest unveiled its twenty-fifth anniversary plane, *Silver One*. The celebration theme was "Still Nuts After All These Years."

## Tried Like Hell

Following deregulation, Southwest's advertising agency asked Kelleher, "Herb, [now that] everybody's free to fly where they want to and charge what they want to, what is it about Southwest

Airlines that we can market?" Kelleher responded, "We've got one thing that's very special; we've got one thing that the other carriers do not have, and that is our people, because we have the most wonderful people in the industry" (Kelleher 1997). This reinforced an earlier statement: "Southwest Airlines is a crusade. If we go another thousand years, I want our people to say this was the finest moment, the finest group of people, the finest institution we've ever had" (Brinkley 1993).

When asked what epitaph he wanted placed on his tombstone, Kelleher replied, "Tried like hell!" This statement is amplified in his favorite adage: "If you are going to light the way for others, you first have to set fire to yourself." He continued, "What people want most in life is to be important to somebody" ("Herb Kelleher Speaks on Leadership" n.d.). At Southwest they are.

## Dancing with His Opposite

Dancing with his opposite comes naturally to Kelleher. His profile highlights him as dominated by culturist ideas. Yet Kelleher also plays the roles of humanist, politicist, and rationalist effectively. His ability to balance the four is represented by his balanced Adam and Eve.

Kelleher's ability to embrace his opposite is reinforced in his long-standing relationship with Colleen Barrett. She describes Kelleher's main contribution as "treat[ing] everyone with love and respect until they give [him] reason not to" (Engler 1990, p. 22). Barrett, reflecting on Kelleher's management side, says, "Herb is the public relations arm of the company, and Colleen runs the day to day operations" (Culture Day 1996). Another official sums up their relationship as "They've worked together so many years, it's like Herb's one side of the brain and she's the other" (McCartney 1995, p. 7).

Barrett notwithstanding, when he struggled early on to get Southwest off the ground, Kelleher was forced to function as both rationalist and politicist, proving that his culturist and humanist dimensions were in harmony with their opposites internally. Barrett brought even more balance externally.

# OPRAH WINFREY:
# A CULTURIST IN ENTERTAINMENT

*"Girl! Look at you! You're not on the farm in Mississippi*
*feeding those chickens no more!"*

(Mair 1994, pp. 96–97)

Few people qualify as cultural icons, and of those who do, not many enjoy the lofty status of billionaire. One such icon, a young black woman recognized around the globe simply as "Oprah," sits atop a billion-dollar business empire and is ranked 427th among the world's wealthiest people. As chief executive of Harpo Inc. ("Oprah" spelled backward), Oprah wears many hats: talk-show host, publishing czar, movie mogul, spiritual guru, educator, philanthropist, and workshop host (Clemetson 2001, pp. 41–43).

So powerful is the name, young people believe that being "Oprah'd" is having to come clean with secrets. Their parents go even further: "Oprahfication," in addition to being a therapeutic process, means "nothing less than the wholesale makeover of the nation, and then the world" (Lowe 1998, pp. 3, 4). One writer sums up the phenomenon: "Oprah Winfrey arguably has more influence on culture than any university president, politician, or religious leader, except perhaps the pope" (pp. xi–xii).

Critics see it differently. They denounce Oprah's "practicing psychotherapy without a license." Criticizing her motivational workshops, they see someone "in the pulpit without ordination" (Donahue 2001, p. D1). Opposing views notwithstanding, the opinion of millions, as summed up by Fran Leibowitz, is that Oprah is "almost a religion" (Lowe 1998, p. 1).

Oprah is a modern-day priestess whose mission is to share how she went to the depths and returned. She overcame what most would consider insurmountable obstacles on a journey from a little farm in Mississippi to reach the zenith of the television world. By sharing her story, Oprah inspires others to search for meaning, self-reliance, and preservance in their lives. "You are responsible for your own life," she reminds them (Sellers 2002, p. 54). Her profile in Figure 15 highlights her symbolic role.

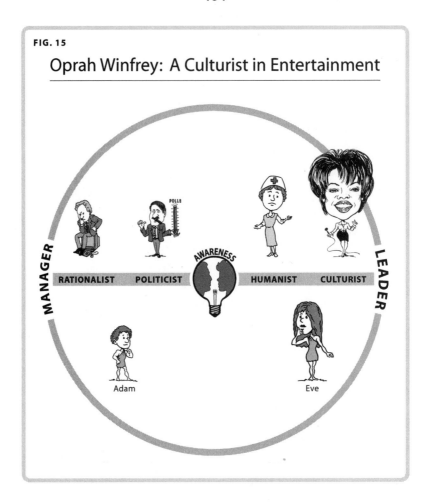

FIG. 15

## Oprah Winfrey: A Culturist in Entertainment

RATIONALIST   POLITICIST   AWARENESS   HUMANIST   CULTURIST

MANAGER

LEADER

POLLS

Adam

Eve

## Outhouse to Penthouse

As one of three finalists in a beauty pageant, Oprah once impressed the judges with her candor. Asked how she would spend a million dollars, the first young lady said she would take care of her parents. The second said she would provide for the poor. Oprah blurted out, "If I had a million dollars . . . I'd be a spending fool!" (Mair 1994, p. 31).

Whether at the outhouse on her grandparents' Mississippi farm or in her luxurious penthouse overlooking Lake Michigan, Oprah lays it on the line. After moving into her fifty-seventh-floor high-rise apartment, Oprah peered into an imaginary mirror and exclaimed, "Girl! Look at you! You're not on the farm in Mississippi feeding those chickens no more!" (pp. 96–97).

Oprah has overcome the difficulties of being both female and black to reach the pinnacle of the entertainment world. One personal challenge remains: She continually struggles with being overweight in a society obsessed with being thin. Oprah regularly reveals her feelings in a society dominated by norms of rationality. Yet on her journey from feeding chickens to overseeing a flourishing empire, she continues to love when it would be easier to hate.

## Oprah and Harpo

Oprah is often described as having two sides: One is her "Oprah" side; the other, "Harpo." "Oprah" reflects her spontaneous, empathic, empowering persona. "Harpo" symbolizes her no-nonsense, shrewd, in-control tendencies (Lowe 1998). Oprah is chair of Harpo Inc., which encompasses *The Oprah Winfrey Show*; O, the Oprah magazine; Harpo Films; and "Live Your Best Life" Workshop Tour (Sellers 2002). Oprah's other assets include a stake in Oxygen Media (a women's cable company), an interest in King World (her show's syndicator, now part of Viacom), five homes, and a vast portfolio of financial investments.

The tension between twins Oprah and Harpo explains why selling any aspect of her diverse conglomerate runs contrary to Oprah's business instincts. She explains, "If I lost control of the business, I'd lose myself—or at least the ability to be myself. Owning myself is a way to be myself."

One writer believes mistakes in Oprah's personal life could tarnish her public image. This could be devastating to Harpo. Anticipating this, Oprah insists all employees sign a lifelong agreement prohibiting their disclosing the inner workings of Harpo. Former employees have failed in their attempts to contest the agreement's legality.

Oprah's description of Harpo's production company applies to her entire empire: "We have created a truly independent, vertically integrated production company. We own our facility; we do our own development. We have the wherewithal, both financially and creatively, to go into any area we want. It will be as big as we want it to be, depending on what we want to do" (Lowe 1998, p. 62).

## By "the Gut"

Managing by instinct rather than by numbers is how Oprah built her entertainment empire. She confesses her inability to understand balance sheets and says "people would fall out of their chairs laughing" were she to convene a strategy meeting (Sellers 2002, p. 58). Describing her decisions as "leaps of faith," Oprah filters advice offered by her staff through her gut instincts. She then trusts her staff to tell her what to do—as long as it fits her own intuition.

Management by the seat of the pants? Hardly. Harpo is anything but a loosely run company. Oprah's hands-on approach creates the perception that she is a "control freak"; for instance, she demands explanations for every corporate expenditure and personally endorses checks written for more than $1,000 (Lowe 1998).

Oprah's "loose-tight" tendencies also appear in her personal life. She confesses to stashing $50 million in her "bag-lady fund" because she was wary of investing it (Sellers 2002). Yet she often goes on spending sprees. One year she spent $2 million on her farm; $1 million for jewelry, $500,000 for gowns, and $130,000 for shoes and purses; $200,000 for horses; $500,000 for vacations; $4 million on her luxury apartment; and $1 million for five fur coats (Mair 1994). Oprah is just as lavish with money she spends on friends and with gifts directed to her favorite charities.

Even though she understands the importance of the nuts-and-bolts aspects of the entertainment business, people are her focus (Lowe 1998). Having once been an employee, she plays the role of employer with a great deal of empathy. She understands what it's like to be called on the carpet. Thus, a sense of fairness weighs heavily on her every action.

When it comes to dealing with people, Oprah seeks an answer to one pivotal question: "Can I trust you?" (Sellers 2002, p. 60). An investment banker representing Oprah when Harpo purchased an interest in Oxygen Media says, "It's all about character with

Oprah. . . . With Oprah, it's like someone is looking into your soul" (p. 60).

### The "Odd Couple"

So different they're called the "odd couple," Oprah and Jeff Jacobs run Harpo. But who is "the man behind the woman"? For helping her set up Harpo in 1986, Oprah gave Jacobs, then an entertainment lawyer, a 5 percent stake in the company. When he joined Harpo as president in 1989, she gave him another 5 percent interest (Sellers 2002).

Although strategic planning is his forte, Jacobs can be tough when it comes to negotiating deals. Referring to Jacobs as "a piranha," Oprah says, "that's a good thing for me to have." Yet the tension between the two can become quite charged. During one planning session, Jacobs suggested, "Let's figure out how we can come up with the next Oprah." Oprah, as though grabbing the suggestion before it reached her ears, replied, "We didn't figure out how to come up with this one! If we had sat in a room and planned this, we never would have created what we have." Rather than splitting their alliance, such exchanges seem to solidify the relationship "between [Oprah] the gut-driven chairman and [Jacobs] the wily president" (Sellers 2002, p. 58).

## Multiple Pulpits

Talking came naturally to Oprah. "When I was three years old, people would tell my grandmother, 'Hattie Mae, this girl sho' can talk'" (Winfrey 2000, p. 57). Kids in her grandmother's church mockingly called her "The Preacher" or "Miss Jesus" (Mair 1994, p. 8). In their wildest imagination, Oprah's early critics could never have envisioned a nationally syndicated television show emcee, a best-selling editor, or a popular workshop leader (Donahue 2001).

### The Oprah Winfrey Show

"It's my soul. It's who I am" (Sellers 2002, p. 60). This is how Oprah describes her long-running talk show, the centerpiece of

Harpo enterprises. When she says "I'm every woman," Oprah speaks from experience:

> The reason I communicate with all these people is because I think I'm every woman and I've had every malady and I've been on every diet and I've had men who have done me wrong, honey. So I related to all of that. And I'm not afraid or ashamed to say it. So whatever is happening, if I can relate to it personally, I always do. (Mair 1994, p. 100)

Relating spiritually is what makes Oprah "the Queen of Talk." She is convinced that her "deep, divine purpose" is to help others find their way, their truth (Harrison 1989, p. 130). As she told Ellen DeGeneres (when DeGeneres went public about being a lesbian), "I simply wanted to support you in being what you believe is the truth for yourself" (Lowe 1998, p. 41).

Oprah describes her beginnings: "I was conceived out of wedlock to Vernon Winfrey and Vernita Lee, who happened by an oak tree one April afternoon in 1953. . . . Their one-time union, not at all a romance, brought about the unwanted pregnancy that was me" (Winfrey 2001, p. 194). Promiscuous at an early age, Oprah was never sure who fathered her own child, a pregnancy that ended in miscarriage when she was fourteen (Mair 1994).

Added to these early emotional scars are the shame and guilt caused by relatives who sexually abused her. "There's only one way I've been able to survive being raped, molested, whipped, rejected . . . only one way to cope with fears of pregnancy, my mother on welfare, my being fat and unpopular. . . . My faith in God got me through" (Lowe 1998, p. 120).

Oprah's early television shows, like those of competitors, sensationalized the darker side of human nature. But in 1994 Oprah did an about-face, "chang[ing] her show's focus from dysfunction to self-actualization." She explained, "TV will no longer use me; I will use TV for my purposes" (Donahue 2001, p. D2). Instead of talking about sex, drugs, and homicides, regular fare of daytime talk shows, Oprah began to focus on human nature's brighter side.

Through Oprah's Angel Network, in 1997 she began underwriting the "Use Your Life Award," offering financial assistance to those who bring meaning to others or take ethical stands that might be politically incorrect. One show featured Roger Boisjoly, the engineer who stood alone in opposing the fateful *Challenger* space launch.

In many ways, Oprah's show mirrors her personal journey from a tumultuous, promiscuous childhood into mature, altruistic womanhood. The show's metamorphosis has been from the sensational to the spiritual. Oprah says, "A good talk show will stimulate thought, present new ideas, and maybe give you a sense of hope where there wasn't any—a feeling of encouragement, enlightenment; inspire you" (Lowe 1998, p. 151). Some of those "new ideas" are captured through Oprah's book club.

**Oprah's Book Club**
Pulitzer Prizes may be coveted by authors, but "Oprahs" are often more profitable (Chin and Cheakalos 1999). "Oprahs" tend to dramatically increase readership and thus authors' royalties. Oprah's monthly book club, begun in 1996, focused on authors whose works Oprah believed "encourage and enlighten" the human spirit. All forty-eight books she promoted on her television show reached best-seller status (Donahue 2003, p. D1). An Oprah Book Club decal on a book's jacket usually increased sales tenfold (Sellers 2002). Nonetheless, Oprah discontinued her book club in 2002, stating, "It has become harder and harder to find books on a monthly basis that I feel absolutely compelled to share" (Donahue 2003, p. D1).

Now, almost a year later, a rejuvenated Oprah plans to resurrect her popular book club, but with a different focus and a new theme: "Traveling with the Classics." She says, "My hope is *The Oprah Winfrey Show* will make classic works of literature accessible to every woman and man who reads" (www.oprah.com). To provide background for the three to five classics selected each year, Oprah plans to originate her show from a locale connected in some way with each book—for example, the author's place of birth or the story's setting. "A gift to myself" is how Oprah describes her decision to emphasize the classics (Donahue 2003, p. D1). And if the past is an indicator of the future, the classics will be resurrected and rise to the top of America's reading lists.

### *O* Magazine

First appearing in April 2000, *O* has set circulation records, outselling stalwarts such as *Vogue* and *Vanity Fair* (Clemetson 2001). *O* is described as "a glossy rendering of Winfrey's on-air motivational crusade. It encourages readers to revamp their souls the way Martha Stewart helps them revamp kitchens" (p. 40). The magazine is read by some 2.5 million subscribers, making it the most successful magazine launch in history (Sellers 2002).

Oprah's priority of "put[ting] the readers first" separates her from most publishers. A typical magazine forces readers to wade through page after page of advertising before they arrive at the table of contents; *O*'s contents appear on page two.

The magazine's centerpiece is "This Month's Mission," which directs readers in their search for meaning. Recent mission statements include "Stepping Out of the Box," "Letting Go," "Journey," "Trust," "Reinvention," "Freedom," "Truth," and "Fun1." Oprah describes her monthly magazine as a personal growth manual.

### "Live Your Best Life" Workshops

Oprah has recently taken her personal development gospel on the road. Like her show and magazine, her workshops are already a success. A recent "Live Your Best Life" workshop in Baltimore illustrates just how far the young "Miss Jesus" has come from Mississippi where her friends poked fun (Donahue 2001, p. D2). It's safe to say, those same friends "ain't makin' fun of her today."

The sold-out Baltimore event drew 1,600 attendees, most of whom were women paying $185 per ticket. Members of the audience "opened their canvas workshop bags, which held journals filled with inspirational thoughts and various exercises. For example, write out 25 negative and 25 positive beliefs about yourself. Winfrey says "we are what we believe" (p. D2). As in her other "pulpits," Oprah told stories about "her grandmother, her love for talking and reading, her years at a Baltimore television station where they told her that her nose, her hair, and her mouth were all wrong."

Like other great leaders, Oprah has never shied away from taking responsibility. She challenges readers of *O* to find meaning in their personal journey: "Your life is a journey of learning to love yourself first and extending that love to others in every encounter" (Winfrey 2001, p. 194). Continuing, she amplifies her admonition:

> Even if you lived through a childhood more challenging than my own, there is one irrefutable law of the universe: We are each responsible for our own life—no other person is or ever can be. Like me, you might have experienced things that caused you to judge yourself unworthy. It's important to know why and how you were programmed to feel the way you do so you can do the work of changing the program. (p. 194)

Oprah empowers people to change their personal programming. On *The Oprah Winfrey Show*, in *O*, and through "Live Your Best Life" workshops, Oprah is like a preacher. She has learned that preaching a thousand different sermons is not as effective as preaching one sermon to a thousand. Her message is consistent and clear: You can change the program of your life. This is the kind of awareness Oprah raises in millions of people.

## Dancing with Her Opposite

Recall that upon moving into her fifty-seventh-floor high-rise apartment, Oprah said, "Girl! Look at you! You're not on the farm in Mississippi feeding those chickens no more!" These are the words of a culturist, a visionary, who, following her dreams, rose not only to the top of a luxurious apartment building but also to the top of a highly profitable entertainment empire.

When Oprah says her employees would fall out of their chairs laughing if she called a strategy meeting, she is speaking the truth.

Still, Oprah is nobody's fool. Her intuition led her to hire Jeff Jacobs, a tough strategist whose wily style seems to complement her own. Oprah recognized what she lacked: a "piranha" to attack the details of Harpo. In effect, when Oprah and Jacobs map Harpo's future, Oprah is dancing with her opposite.

Oprah's talk show, magazine, and workshops highlight her humanism. Few doubt Oprah's dedication to helping people, particularly the less fortunate. Her humanist leanings, coupled with her culturist instincts, explain why her Eve is so large. Can she dance with her opposite?

In her relationship with Jacobs, she makes the dance with her rationalist side external. But the fact that she admittedly can't read balance sheets or call strategy meetings implies that she is not comfortable with her inner rationalist side. Balancing her strong culturist and humanist orientations internally with her weaker rationalist and politicist leanings might make Oprah an even more comfortable CEO. Then again, who can dispute her success as she is?

# RONALD REAGAN:
# A CULTURIST IN THE PRESIDENCY

*"The greatest leader is not necessarily the one who does the greatest things;*
*he is the one that gets the people to do the greatest things."*

(A&E *Biography* Video, Oct. 14, 1998)

Ronald Reagan was sworn in as the nation's fortieth president in a setting strongly conveying that symbolism would permeate his presidency. An imposing Capitol building provided a backdrop; awe-inspiring memorials to Washington, Jefferson, and Lincoln stood out in the foreground; and his mother's well-worn Bible supported his right hand as he took the oath. A building, three memorials, a Bible: Each told a story.

That January day in 1980, Americans observed the beginnings of what one writer termed "the politics of symbolism" (Dallek 1984). By turning his back to the Capitol, Reagan was reiterating what he had said throughout his campaign: "I'm against big government." By symbolically paying tribute to three widely acclaimed presidents, Reagan was reaffirming their legacy. America was determined to remain forever free, a destiny Reagan believed included winning the Cold War. By placing his left hand on his mother's Bible, Reagan was reassuring the world that conservative values learned at her knee would guide his administration.

That the Bible opened to a verse reflecting one of those early lessons is of no small significance: "If my people, which are called by my name, shall humble themselves, and pray, and seek my face, and turn from their wicked ways; then will I hear from heaven, and will forgive their sin, and will heal their land" (2 Chronicles 7:14). In the margin, Nelle Reagan wrote, "A most wonderful verse for the healing of the nations" (Noonan 2001, p. 161). Reagan's driving passion was to bring "healing" to America while delivering the world from the "wicked ways" of the "Evil Empire" (the Soviet Union).

As though reciting a memorized script, Reagan captures the imagined moment: "Standing here, one faces a magnificent vista. . . . At the end of the mall are those shrines to the giants on whose shoulders we stand" (Bosch 1998, p. 142). In effect, he was launching his presidency with the same positive outlook of roles played in countless Western films. He would be "a friend, a pal, a guy to reassure us that the story is going to come out all right" (Barber 1992, p. 227).

As president, Reagan wanted more than anything to be seen as a hero. As a young lifeguard, he rescued struggling swimmers. In Hollywood, he played roles in which he rescued people in distress. Edmund Morris, his biographer, describes this heroic yearning:

> I think he felt sincerely in his heart that he was rescuing the United States from a period of poisonous self-doubt, loss of direction, loss of belief in itself. I think he felt in the late 1970s that he could rescue Jimmy Carter's America and carry her back to the shore and make her alive again. (in Bosch 1998, p. 124)

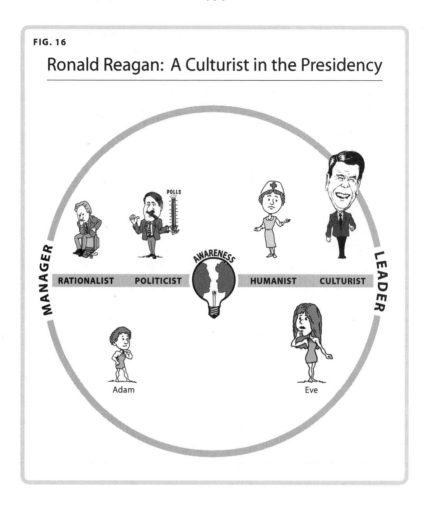

**FIG. 16**

## Ronald Reagan: A Culturist in the Presidency

Reagan concurs: "I'm a sucker for hero worship" (Reagan with Huber 1965, p. 35). The consummate culturist, Reagan is clearly on the right side of the model in Figure 16.

## The Great Storyteller

Great leaders tell good stories, and no one could tell a better one than Ronald Reagan. Biographers refer to him as the "Great Communicator." But more than rhetoric contributed to his reputation as a storyteller. He explains his unique ability: "I never thought it was my style or the words I used that made a difference: It was the content. I wasn't a great communicator, but I communicated great things, and they didn't spring full bloom from my brow; they came from the heart of a great nation" (Reagan, 1998, p. 20).

Reagan took mundane events and, with a little artistic embellishment, created in the imaginations of others a sense of being present in the moment. Consider the patriotic spin he gave the circumstances surrounding his birth: "My face was blue from screaming, my bottom was red from whacking, and my father claimed . . . he was white" (Reagan with Huber 1965, p. 3).

## The Power of Pretending

Describing Reagan's early preparation for Hollywood, J. David Barber writes, "Long before he became a professional actor, he had trained in pretending: that he really could see the blackboard, that his father was not really drunk, that he really could play football, that he really did belong in the rich kids' crowd" (1992, p. 253).

In his autobiography, Reagan reconstructs circumstances that amplify Barber's assessment. "I sat in the front row at school and still could not read the blackboard" (p. 19). Reagan is referring to his poor eyesight; he compensated by pretending he could see as well as anyone.

"I wanted to let myself in the house and go to bed and pretend he wasn't there" (p. 7). Here Reagan is describing finding his father in a drunken stupor on the front porch. It was a scene that inspired his politics of independence.

"At my size—five foot three and weighing 108 pounds—scrimmage was denied me, but I never missed a practice" (p. 19). Reagan is recalling his attempts to play football, a dream he eventually realized.

"Lifeguarding provides one the best vantage points in the world to learn about people" (p. 21). Here Reagan is recalling one of the loves of his life. As a lifeguard Reagan met and socialized with the leisure class, a group that eventually influenced his political thinking as he moved from the governorship of California to the presidency of the United States.

### Eureka

Reflecting on becoming aware of his way with words, Reagan recalled a student revolt at his alma mater, Eureka College. Speaking to a large gathering of students and faculty, Reagan sensed the hold he had over his audience:

> I discovered that night that an audience has a feel to it and, in the parlance of the theater, that audience and I were together. When I came to actually presenting the motion there was no need for parliamentary procedure: they came to their feet with a roar—even the faculty members present voted for the acclamation. It was heady wine. Hell, with two more lines I could have had them riding through "every Middlesex village and farm"—without horses yet. (Reagan with Huber 1965, pp. 28–29)

Throughout his two terms in office, Reagan had most Americans riding along. Daughter Maureen explains why. "Ronald Reagan's greatest accomplishment really was being Ronald Reagan. . . . It was the fact that he made us believe in ourselves . . . at a time . . . when we thought we were losing the 'Cold War.' . . . [He said] there's nothing we can't solve; we're Americans" (Matthews 1999). Reagan offers another interpretation. During his campaign for the California governorship he was asked, "What is it that people see in you?" He answered with a self-effacing question, "Would you laugh if I told you that they look at me and they see themselves?" (Bosch 1998, p. 14). In effect, Ronald Reagan personified "the nation's most cherished myths" (p. 19).

## Reagan's Style: Hands Off

Reagan's style departed from that of Nixon, Ford, and Carter. He led and they managed. Nowhere is this distinction more evident than in the Cold War. Whereas predecessors saw "the Soviet-American confrontation . . . as a competition to be managed," Reagan saw it "as a moral struggle between good and evil" (Bosch 1998, p. 199).

Because Reagan delegated the day-to-day tasks of the presidency, *Fortune* suggested that CEOs should emulate his hands-off style. It is a style Barber describes as being that of a passive positive. "Passive-positive types help soften the harsh edges of politics. But their dependence and the fragility of their hopes and enjoyments make disappointment in politics likely" (Barber 1992, p. 10).

For all intents and purposes, three men ran the Oval Office under Reagan's watch: James Baker, Edwin Meese, and Michael Deaver. The three "deputy presidents" formed Reagan's "troika" (Bosch 1998). Maureen explains, "Ronald Reagan's operating style has always been 'bring me all the options.' Lay them on the table. Get your best advocates. I want to hear them argue about it and then hopefully I will make the right decision" (p. 275).

### The Iran-Contra Affair

Reagan's hands-off style had its downside. Overdelegating got him into trouble in the Iran-Contra affair. If he knew about the arms-for-hostages trade-off, he lied to the American people. If he was unaware, he was asleep at the switch. On a matter of this magnitude, no CEO, let alone the president of the United States, should permit the final decision to be made by others.

The hostage affair brought to light another flaw in Reagan's style: an inclination to gloss over details. One writer traces this tendency back to Reagan's alcoholic father, Jack: "Reagan is a classic model of the successful child of an alcoholic: he doesn't hear things and doesn't see things that he doesn't want to hear and see" (Bosch 1998, p. 296). Reagan's speech following the arms-for-hostages fiasco supports this point: "A few months ago, I told the American people I did not trade arms for hostages. My heart and my best intentions still tell me that's true, but the facts and the evidence tell me it is not" (p. 308).

In an attempt to tighten the looseness occasionally creeping into the White House, Reagan hired Donald Regan as chief of staff. Regan, retired CEO of Merrill Lynch, was a tough-talking former Marine. Whereas Reagan was very much hands-off, Regan was very heavy handed. He believed he could "make 85 percent of the decisions" Reagan made (p. 302). But Regan's abrasive manner irritated Nancy Reagan. Her disdain for the power-obsessed chief of staff reached a breaking point when he hung up on her during a phone conversation. Regan was gone the next day.


### The Evil Empire

In fairy tales, heroes typically encounter dragons that must be slain. Usually the dragon has captured a young damsel, and her distress inspires the hero to heights of reality-defying bravery. For Reagan, the Soviet Union was the cruel dragon and the United States represented the endangered damsel.

"Mr. Gorbachev, tear down this wall" are words permanently imprinted on the American psyche. Ronald Reagan made the memorable statement as he stood outside the Brandenberg Gate challenging his Russian counterpart to join him in ending the Cold War. Later, when the wall came down, Reagan had a portion of it placed on the lawn of his library. To him it symbolized his Cold War victory. When asked about his father's legacy, Michael Reagan confirmed this view: "The big piece of the Berlin Wall before his library. That's his legacy" (McFeaters 1999, p. D6). Columnist George Will echoed these sentiments but gave them a different twist: "If you seek his monument, look around at what you don't see; you don't see the Berlin Wall; you don't see the Iron Curtain" (Bosch 1998, p. 20).

Reagan triumphed in his battle with the "Evil Empire" by doing what other great leaders do. He convinced followers to join him in a battle against evil. He continually stressed that America was committed to a nuclear defense system regardless of the costs in either dollars or world opinion. Reagan prevailed in his "war of words" with Gorbachev.

When Russian dissident Anatoly Shcharansky met Reagan at the White House, he "told him that his speech about the Evil Empire was a great encourager for us. . . . Star Wars was a way of talking to the Soviet Union! And he linked the fate of dissidents to the policy of the United States of America" (Noonan 2001, p. 214).

## Debating Carter and Mondale

What do a peanut farmer and a former movie star have in common? Very little, and the 1980 debate between Carter and Reagan proves the point, particularly if one focuses on their contrasting political styles. Carter, the "Great Articulator" armed with facts, squared off against Reagan, the "Great Communicator" armed with words. Three pivotal moments occurred during the debate and Reagan quickly turned them to his advantage.

The first incident concerned a statement Carter had made to his teenage daughter prior to the debate. "I had a discussion with my daughter, Amy . . . to ask her what she thought the most important issue was. She said she thought nuclear weaponry and the conrol of arms" ("Carter-Reagan Debate" 1980, p. 15). A feeble attempt to portray Reagan as a warmonger, Carter's use of Amy backfired. "Ask Amy" signs began to appear across the nation (Cannon 1982, p. 296).

The second incident involved Reagan's memorable "there you go again" response to Carter's charge that he did not support Medicare legislation ("Ronald Reagan" 1998). Reagan argued that he did not support socialized medicine. Regarding his impromptu response, Reagan said,

> I think there was some pent-up anger in me over Carter's claims that I was a racist and warmonger. Just as he'd distorted my view on states' rights and arms control, he had distorted it regarding Medicare, and my response just burst out of me spontaneously. The audience loved it and I think Carter added to the impact of the words by looking a little sheepish on the television screen." (Reagan 1990, p. 221)

The third incident in the debate illustrates this point. Reagan asked the American people, "Are you better off than you were four years ago?" He amplified his general query with several specific ones. Is it easier to buy things? Is there more, or less, unemployment? Is America respected throughout the world? And, is the country as strong as it was four years ago? "If you answer all those questions yes," Reagan nodded toward Carter and said, "then I think your choice is very obvious." Then, sensing that he had an open-and-shut case, Reagan donned the "white hat" he wore in the movies and, in true Western style, told Americans that "If you don't agree, I could suggest another choice that you have" (Commission on Presidential Debates; Debate Transcripts). Biographer Lou Cannon summed up the debate: "What was on display that October night in Cleveland, as in the Carter and Reagan presidencies, were different types of intelligence" (Cannon 1991, p. 141).

Later, in his second debate with challenger Walter Mondale, Reagan appeared tired and out of sync with the process. He seemed to lack his usual "I'm-in-command" presence. However, he came to life when a panelist asked him if he was up to handling an emergency like the Cuban missile crisis, one that required long hours and youthful courage like that of John Kennedy. Reagan responded as if reading for a part in another movie: "I will not make age an issue of this campaign. I am not going to exploit, for political purposes, my opponent's youth and experience" (Mondale was much younger). Mondale, who felt that he had won their first debate, told his wife that his aspirations for the White House ended with the audience's enthusiastic response to Reagan's showmanship ("Ronald Reagan" 1998).

## The Real Reagan: On the Bench or on the Screen?

To have observed Reagan play football in real life at Eureka College and on the screen at Notre Dame would deepen one's understanding of just how difficult it is to distinguish Reagan the person from Reagan the actor. It doesn't seem overreaching to conclude that Reagan himself may have encountered difficulty making the distinction.

In his collegiate days at Eureka, Reagan's attitude was that of the gung-ho jock, playing little yet never missing a practice. In the movie *Knute Rockne—All American,* Reagan's attitude was quite different, bordering on defiance. Playing the part of George Gipp, Reagan was the culmination of a vision Rockne shared with some of his players: "a halfback who can carry the mail, a big fast boy who can run, pass, and kick like, say, Jim Thorpe."

In real life Reagan mostly sat on the bench, but in film he was transformed into Notre Dame's fleet-footed halfback who led the Irish to one victory after another. Yet the most memorable scene in the movie occurs as his character Gipp is dying. He tells Rockne, standing by his bedside, to remind the team, when breaks are going against them, "to win one for the Gipper." These words are permanently etched in filmgoers' memory. Reagan continually evoked their spirit in his reign as president.

Reagan's role in the film later took on a life of its own. He visited Notre Dame in 1988 for the centennial celebration of Rockne's birth. The unveiling of a postage stamp with the legendary coach's image marked the occasion (Sperber 1998). In *Onward to Victory*, Murray Sperber, drawing on the observations of historian Gary Wills, points out how the spirit of Rockne permeated Reagan's political career:

> He not only portrayed himself as the Gipper but also as Rockne, that in essence his political addresses, particularly as president, were locker-room speeches to the nation, invoking the past, explaining the present, and challenging Americans to go out there and win the future. The March 1988 talk at Notre Dame contained such pep-talk lines as "I happen to have always believed in the American people. Don't sell them short. Given the proper tools and a level playing ground, our workers can outproduce and outcompete anyone, anywhere." (1998, p. 25)

When Reagan spoke at Notre Dame, a banner hung behind the platform from which he spoke; it read, "Notre Dame Welcomes the Gipper" (p. 25). As Sperber points out, not only did Reagan believe he was the Gipper, but he also believed he was Rockne. From his birth in Tampico to the day he stood before the Berlin Wall, Reagan was ever the actor. Only the scripts changed. His own observation about the presidency proved that he had trouble distinguishing himself from his fictional roles: "There have been times . . . when I have wondered how you could do the job [serve as president] if you hadn't been an actor" (Bosch 1998, p. 8).

## Full Circle

Reagan excelled in painting word pictures. Breaking with tradition, he had been sworn in on the west side of the Capitol where he could "look west, toward Illinois, where he had been born, and California, where he had become a public figure" (Noonan 2001, p. 160).

Reagan left the presidency as he entered: telling stories. While in office, he had continually embellished the "City on a Hill" metaphor to lift American spirits. As he said farewell, he gave a "State of the City" update.

> And how stands the city on this winter night? More prosperous, more secure, and happier than it was eight years ago. But more than that; after two hundred years, two centuries, she still stands strong and true on the granite ridge, and her glow has held steady no matter what storm. And she's still a beacon, still a magnet for all who must have freedom, for all the pilgrims from all the lost places who are hurtling through the darkness, toward home. (p. 316)

## Dancing with His Opposite

In *When Character Was King,* Peggy Noonan writes, "Ronald Reagan did not so much have the natural talents and cast of mind of a businessman or economist or political figure; he had the natural talents and cast of mind of an artist" (2001, p. 38). She explains that he loved "drawing faces, caricatures and cartoons, designing leather crafts and memorizing poetry" (p. 38).

Reagan's caricature is situated on the right side of the model because he painted word pictures using symbols, metaphors, and stories. Reagan's Eve supports his culturist leanings. As a hands-off leader, Reagan had trouble dancing with his rational opposite. He attempted to correct this imbalance by hiring tough, bottom-line-oriented Donald Regan. But hiring Regan was a fiasco. He was unable to get along with people, particularly Nancy Reagan. Reagan also attempted to dance with his "deputy presidents," Baker, Meese, and Deaver. They were charged with running the day-to-day affairs of the executive branch. Although more successful at embracing his troika than Regan, Reagan still seemed to encounter difficulties integrating his rational and spiritual sides.

Reagan was a brilliant leader but not a great manager. He led America to victory in the Cold War but allowed himself to become embroiled in an illegal arms sale he failed to manage. Few doubt that Reagan the culturist is one of our great presidents. But the question remains: Would historians write even grander things about his presidency had he been able to be more at home with his rationalist side?

## THREE PROFILES, ONE STYLE

Consider the profiles of these three leaders. Do you see yourself leading like Kelleher, Oprah, or Reagan?

- Are you prone to focus on providing your enterprise purpose and meaning?
- Do you use symbols, metaphors, and stories to convey meanings that touch the human spirit?
- Do you champion rituals and celebrations?

If so, the culturist profile probably personifies your dominant style. Let's review the three leaders' profiles.

### Kelleher

Kelleher's caricature reflects a focus on building meaning into Southwest's way of doing things. He champions rituals, ceremonies, and celebrations. From arm wrestling for the right to use the slogan "Just Plane Smart" to being Southwest's lead rapper, Herb Kelleher dances with Southwest's unions, pilots, flight attendants, and service personnel, creating a culture that is the envy of the industry.

Kelleher's feminine side, his Eve, supports his more dominant culturist, and humanist, leanings. However, Kelleher was a highly successful CEO because his robust Adam indicates an ability to deal effectively with rationalist and politicist logic.

Now retired, Kelleher is arguably one of the most successful CEOs in aviation history. When you observe him in action, you may join Gordon Bethune in concluding, "He's larger than life. I've never met anyone who didn't like Herb Kelleher" (Jones 2001, p. B5).

## Winfrey

Oprah's caricature is positioned on the right side of the continuum, reflecting her culturist and humanist leanings. Oprah's Eve supports her position while indicating her struggle with her Adam's rationalist and politicist sides.

What's the key to Oprah's icon status? Frankly, Oprah is proud of who she is—"a twofer" (Mair 1994)—an African American woman whose tragedies and triumphs add depth to her culturist and humanist leanings. Even though she is not fully integrated or balanced internally, Oprah continues to inspire people. She is also smart enough to balance her weaknesses with Jacobs, her counterpart. Her life story is proof that her sermons originate in the school of hard knocks, not in a textbook. When she exclaimed, "Look at you, girl!" Oprah summed up her journey from a chicken farm in Mississippi to the top of the entertainment world.

## Reagan

Ronald Reagan shares the spotlight with Kelleher and Oprah. Though dominated by his culturist side, Reagan was also a humanist. The size of his Eve supports these humanist leanings. Like many effective leaders, Reagan was a master storyteller, using symbols and painting word pictures to reach the American people. "Mr. Gorbachev, tear down this wall" echoes in the nation's history.

Reagan's rationalist alignment was his Achilles' heel, a weakness shown by his smaller Adam. Yet Reagan led the nation to glorious heights. He won the Cold War and, in the process, changed the world's map. His difficulty in balancing his opposite was a thorn in his side throughout his administration. Still, Reagan ranks as one of America's great presidents. His aforementioned vision of a City on a Hill continues to inspire the souls of Americans. It motivated Reagan to lead the nation to what he fervently believed was its God-appointed destiny: occupying that City.

Kelleher, Oprah, and Reagan reached the summit of their respective careers as culturists. While Kelleher seemed to dance effectively with his rational and politicist opposites, Oprah and Reagan encountered difficulties. Nonetheless, all three are effective leaders. Once again, remember that, if you find yourself identifying more easily with the culturist than with the rationalist, politicist, or humanist, you still have aspects of all the orientations. The trick is finding the right balance.

# Challenging Your Reflection

*Your ability to reflect on your style determines how effective you'll be as a manager-leader.*

CHAPTER

**7**

# Reflecting
# While Dancing

Philosophers have long extolled the virtue of self-reflection. Socrates observed that "the unexamined life is not worth living." Dewey agreed that "freedom is the power to choose among known alternatives." More recently, basketball coach Phil Jackson concluded that "awareness is everything" (1995, p. 35). But if awareness is everything, how does it come about? What does awareness feel like? More important, how do you raise your own level of awareness?

In *The Varieties of Religious Experience*, William James speaks of "sudden" and "gradual" ways "in which inner unification may occur" (1902, p. 152). Awareness may be experienced as revolutionary. An event suddenly catapults you into a state of higher consciousness. Or it may happen as an evolutionary series of events gradually raising your consciousness. The following examples illustrate the difference.

As noted earlier, on September 11, 2001, Mayor Rudy Giuliani was thrust into a terrible situation for which he had no time to prepare. Skyscrapers crumbled, people plunged to their deaths, chaos reigned, and Giuliani was forced to change his role. On September 10, New Yorkers had perceived him as a tough, no-nonsense manager whose primary concern was ridding the city of crime. Twenty-four hours later, the world saw him as a caring, compassionate leader. Concern for the emotional welfare of New Yorkers drove him to exhaustion as he attempted to restore some sense of meaning to their lives. In one cataclysmic moment, Giuliani had moved from managing to leading. His awareness level skyrocketed under the suddenly changed circumstances.

Giuliani and his fellow New Yorkers were not alone. The entire nation was jolted into a state of heightened awareness on September 11. What had been a take-it-for-granted optimistic country turned into an alert, apprehensive nation. "Heightened awareness" has become a part of every American's vocabulary. Its symbolic significance, reflected in the crumbling twin towers, is indelibly carved on America's collective psyche.

As a result of the tragic events of that day, symbols and their meanings permeate day-to-day conversations, replacing our preoccupation with mundane routine. Memorial services commemorating the completion of the World Trade towers' cleanup illustrate the point. No politicians spoke. An American flag draped over an empty casket honored firefighters, police officers, and rescue workers who lost their lives. Another American flag was placed over the last steel girder removed from the site. Thousands watched as an ambulance and a tractor-trailer bore the coffin and steel beam away. The ceremony delivered one simple yet profound message: Noble men and women who died were gone but not forgotten.

Awareness is not always so abrupt. In 1972, Title IX, guaranteeing women the same opportunities in athletics as men, became the law of the land. Thirty years later, the battle for equality on the nation's playing fields continues. What was legislated to be a sudden change has become a gradual, ongoing process of seeing inequalities and determining how they might be changed.

In her book *Tilting the Playing Field,* Jessica Gavora refers to the struggle of female athletes as "affirmative androgyny" (2002, p. 9). Like affirmative action related to civil rights legislation, the process of raising the nation's consciousness to the plight of women athletes is evolutionary rather than revolutionary. In fact, Gavora refers to the 1972 act as the codification of the women's movement launched by Betty Friedan and others in the 1960s.

On its thirtieth anniversary, Title IX has come to symbolize the age-old struggle between masculine and feminine. Proponents see "the law as life-altering and empowering" yet "wonder what it says about American culture that women are more easily accepted as doctors and lawyers than pitchers and point guards" (Brady 2002, p. C1). Opponents view it as "a blunt instrument used to kill men's teams." Regardless of the position one assumes in the debate, Title IX and the lawsuits it has generated will continue to raise America's level of awareness bit by bit.

## AN ONGOING PERSONAL ASSESSMENT

A pivotal question raised in this chapter is how to go about increasing our awareness levels. We believe three perspectives define the ongoing process.

1. Looking back into the past and dredging up historical roots, ask these questions:
   - Where did I come from?
   - What childhood experiences strongly affected me?
   - What was my family life like as I grew up?
   - Which teachers, coaches, or other grownups meant the most to me?

2. Analyzing current strengths and weaknesses, ask these questions:
   - Where am I now?
   - What is my dominant style, the one with which I feel most comfortable?
   - What other styles do I struggle with?
   - What leadership qualities have my favorite teachers, coaches, and employers exemplified?

3. Forecasting the future, ask these questions:
   - Where do I need to be to have a satisfying career and good life?
   - When I have encountered difficulties with teachers, employers, and others, was it because I had trouble with their styles?
   - To realize my potential, do I need to appreciate and adopt positive aspects of other styles, even though they clash with mine?

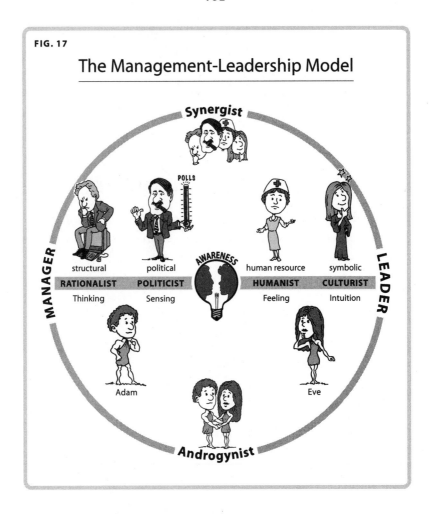

**FIG. 17**

# The Management-Leadership Model

Tough self-reflection requires a personal mirror, one that reflects an accurate image of you, and because it does, helps you identify your possible options. The management-leadership model serves as that mirror. The centerpiece of the model is awareness, symbolized by the lightbulb. As your internal lightbulb lights up, you begin to experience "Aha!" moments, to see things that provoke questions: What is my dominant orientation? What is my opposite? Are my masculine and feminine impulses in harmony? Answers form around time-oriented perspectives: the past, the present, and the future.

## AWARENESS REQUIRES
## A LOOK INTO THE PAST

Management-leadership leanings are scripted early in life. More often than not, childhood's imprint on a manager's or leader's style is profound. In fact, the styles of our profiled leaders can be traced back to early experiences. Consider those of rationalists Crandall, Summitt, and Nixon.

As a young boy, Robert Crandall attended twelve public schools. Because of the insecurity created by the moves, young Crandall found it necessary to continually reestablish his turf. How? Each time, he got into fistfights with other young men. This chip-on-the-shoulder pugnacity followed Crandall into the airline industry and earned him the nickname "Darth Vader."

Pat Summitt grew up driving a tractor on the family farm. Her father expected as much of her as he did of his sons. Hard work was a given. Now at the University of Tennessee, hard work is a given among the Lady Vols. Summitt's players endure practices as tough mentally as physically.

Richard Nixon grew up helping his mother tend the family grocery. There he learned frugality, a trait that later often evoked paranoia toward wealthy people, particularly the Eastern Establishment. Nixon's distrust led him to make self-destructive decisions, Watergate being one of those.

Early scripting is also evident in our politicists. As a young boy, Frank Lorenzo traded stocks. Later, in college, he rigged student elections. Although in different forms, both behaviors would surface again during his airline career. He traded assets as pieces on a chessboard, and in negotiations he always had a hidden agenda, centered around his personal interests.

Early on, Lyndon Johnson recognized the importance of power. As a young boy, he became man of the house when his father traveled. Later, he sought jobs that placed him near centers of influence. From these experiences he learned to build coalitions that enhanced his political agenda.

From the day she punched a neighborhood bully and thereby gained the respect of both her mother and a group of boys who witnessed the blow, Hillary Clinton has been "playing with the boys." Following her mother's admonition to hit back has stood Hillary in good stead in the rough-and-tumble world of a male-dominated Senate.

The humanists, too, developed at a young age. As a boy, Donald Burr was active in convincing neighborhood kids to attend young people's meetings at his church. When Burr founded People Express, he had a simple purpose: freeing workers from corporate bureaucratic prisons. He encouraged employees to think of themselves as owners rather than as commodities.

As a young girl, Betty Friedan was troubled by her mother's lack of ambition. Unlike her mother, she determined she would escape the feminine mystique's confining influence. Many thought her idealism too liberal, even branding her a communist. Yet Friedan was genuinely interested in what women could become, once freed from their culturally ascribed psychic prison. Friedan and others founded NOW to be an instrument for women's rights, equalities she advocated in *The Feminine Mystique*.

Jimmy Carter's parents were strong role models. His father, Earl, taught him the details of running the family peanut farm. His mother, Miss Lillian, nursed him back to health from a life-threatening colon inflammation. As Carter matured, he showed strong rationalist tendencies. Yet, when confronted with major choices, he was ruled more by his heart than by his head.

The culturists also showed early signs of where they would eventually end up. Herb Kelleher grew up listening to stories. During a high school basketball game, Kelleher would not take the shot that would make him the school's all-time scoring leader. He was concerned about his teammates and teamwork. The ability to tell stories, coupled with his unselfish attitude, made Kelleher a legend in the airline industry. His "luv" for people is a driving force behind Southwest Airlines' phenomenal success.

In childhood, Oprah Winfrey's friends mockingly referred to her as "Miss Jesus." Growing up in near poverty, she experienced the difficulties stemming from being born out of wedlock. Today she uses her television program and her O magazine to help others live more meaningful lives.

Ronald Reagan is known as the "Great Communicator." He convinced Americans to believe in themselves at a time of collective self-doubt. As a young boy, he acted in plays conducted by his mother and went with her to church. As a young lifeguard, he took great pride in saving seventy-some swimmers from drowning. His focus as president was to rescue America from the "Evil Empire" by winning the Cold War with the Soviet Union.

Reviewing the childhoods of these twelve people should help you shed light on your own journey into the past. We can't disassociate ourselves from our past, but we can study it and learn from it, seeking to pinpoint how it affects our current approaches to managing and leading.

## AWARENESS REQUIRES A LOOK AT THE PRESENT

We all have our own view of reality, and we assume that how we see things is the best way or, more often than not, the only way. Reflection in action means knowing yourself and owning up to your management and leadership preferences. Too many people in top positions are prisoners of their cognitive assumptions. As a result, they end up making colossal mistakes without fully realizing how and why things went wrong. Witness the *Challenger* disaster, the greed and fraud exposed in corporate scandals, and the controversy surrounding the "New" Coke. The worlds of business, health care, and education are fraught with examples of leaders and managers who were convinced they had it right when they were actually well off the mark.

Hindsight is twenty-twenty, as when Robert McNamara concluded about his management of the war in Vietnam, "We were wrong, terribly wrong." Thinking ahead through multiple views helps us foresee pitfalls and opportunities. Socrates' advice to "know thyself" is as apt today as it was in his day. Unfortunately, most management and leadership programs don't emphasize the inner search. That's why people have to take it upon themselves to expand their cognitive reflections. To aid this personal effort, we return to the model as a mirror and then go to the playground where we find the best teachers of all—children.

## Mirror, Mirror in My Hand

We have stressed the model as a mirror in which to observe strengths and weaknesses of your management-leadership style. One caveat: We did not promise that as you look into the mirror you will discover the fairest manager or leader of them all. However, we do believe you will become aware of the need to balance your internal manager and leader. By overhearing what we call the "awareness talk" of the rationalist, politicist, humanist, and culturist, you will discover your own inner dialogue. Listen to the rationalist and humanist, the culturist and politicist as they dialogue with their opposites.

### The Rationalist and Humanist Opposite

Imagine the following dialogue between the rationalist and his mirror opposite, the humanist, shown as the nurse.

*Rationalist:* Mirror, mirror in my hand, who is the best manager in the land?

*Mirror (with nurse appearing):* My dear rationalist, you have some marvelous points. Precision, details, and the exercise of control are your strengths.

*Rationalist:* Well, what else is there? After all, it's results that count.

*Mirror:* But I see people with long faces. Their needs reach beyond their paychecks. They feel like cogs in a machine, not appreciated as human beings. Frankly, rationalist, you need to become aware of my way of doing things.

*Rationalist:* And what is that?

*Mirror:* Treat people with respect. Tell them how much you appreciate them. In short, show them that they are needed and respected, that they are more than robots in the machinery of production.
*Rationalist:* You make a good point, humanist. No wonder morale is so low around here. I'm on one page, and everyone else is on another. I'm out of balance.

### The Culturist and Politicist Opposite

Similarly, the culturist has a conversation with her mirror opposite, the politicist.

*Culturist:* Mirror, mirror in my hand, who is the best leader in the land?

*Mirror (with politicist appearing):* Ah, Ms. Culturist, your visions are inspiring to say the least. Your intuition and your ability to picture the future, to see around the corner, are mind-boggling!
*Culturist:* My ideas generate change; they encourage people to see the big picture. If it weren't for me, we would still be doing things the way we did fifty years ago.
*Mirror:* But people think you are too heavenly minded to be of any earthly good. You need to get both feet on the ground.
*Culturist:* What do you mean, get both feet on the ground?
*Mirror:* I mean, you need to build coalitions. Resources are limited. If you are to implement your ideas, you need power; without it, your ideas will never get off the ground.
*Culturist:* I believe you're right. I need to become more political and cultivate relationships that support my vision. Thanks for your advice. Even though I have never liked politics, you make me aware of how important they are. Practicality has never been my strong suit.

## Lessons from Ants and Teeter-Totters

King Solomon once advised his sluggish hearers to "go to the ant . . . consider her ways and be wise" (Proverbs 6:6). What did the great king have in mind? By considering the thriftiness of ants—

how they organize, carry loads much larger than themselves, and provide for members of their sprawling communities—his hearers would become aware of their lethargy and, more important, do something about it.

While ants have something to teach us, children may have even more. Go to the playground and consider the play of boys and girls, particularly how they go about balancing their teeter-totters.

What does a teeter-totter have to do with managing and leading? When you plotted your scores on the Locator, you were, in effect, constructing two teeter-totters needing to be balanced (see Figure 18). Now return in your imagination to kids on a playground playing on their teeter-totters.

Let's assume a 150-pound boy (the rationalist in the model) sits on one end and an 80-pound girl (the humanist in the model) sits on the other, as shown in Figure 19. What happens? The girl's end of the teeter-totter rises so high that she cannot touch the ground, while the boy's end sits on the ground. If we transpose this to our model, overemphasis on management calls for the boy and girl to work together until they reach a balance.

**FIG. 18**

## Management-Leadership Teeter-Totters

FIG. 19

## Too Much Management

FIG. 20

## Too Much Leadership

Now imagine an opposite set of circumstances, as shown in Figure 20. When a girl (the culturist in the model) positions herself on one end of the teeter-totter and a much lighter boy (the politicist in the model) positions himself on the other end, the boy's end rises so high he can't touch the ground. Transposed to the model, there is now an overemphasis on leadership. Again working together, they find a balance.

Symbolically speaking, an unbalanced teeter-totter creates the need for awareness. The message is clear: Go to the ant to learn thrift; go to the playground to learn balance.

# AWARENESS REQUIRES A LOOK INTO THE FUTURE

As the world becomes even more complex, organizations will need people who are well integrated, able to operate at the top and bottom of the management-leadership circle. They are the synergist and the androgynist, both of whose abilities to integrate diverse factors are reflected in the practice of alchemists during the Middle Ages.

## The Four Faces of the Synergist

The faces of the rationalist, the politicist, the humanist, and the culturist make up the synergist's image in the model. The rationalist and politicist reflect the more masculine, "left-brain" leanings of management. The humanist and culturist reflect the more feminine, "right-brain" leanings of leadership.

Sometimes opposing left- and right-brain leanings can be integrated in one individual. Herb Kelleher of Southwest Airlines and Phil Jackson, coach of the Lakers basketball team, are examples. Both are equally suited as inspired managers and grounded leaders. In today's social and economic environment, both clarity and spirituality, passion and precision are valuable traits. The gifted synergist is a well-balanced individual who provides meaningful control as well as systematic inspiration. Through awareness, anyone can work toward a harmonic, synergistic balance. But our reach is often greater than our grasp.

Enter the synergistic organization. Tapping people with diverse qualities who can work harmoniously covers the territory without demanding too much of any one person. While the detail-driven operations people may drive the big-picture people crazy, an artful ballet of oppositional players can create a symphonic performance as passion and precision interplay to everyone's benefit. All it takes is an accepting collective awareness where tension among different voices is prized.

## The Archetypal Faces of the Androgynist

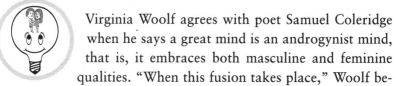

Virginia Woolf agrees with poet Samuel Coleridge when he says a great mind is an androgynist mind, that is, it embraces both masculine and feminine qualities. "When this fusion takes place," Woolf believes, "the mind is fully fertilized and uses all its faculties" (1929, p. 98). Yet she puzzles over whether an androgynist mind is "man-womanly" or "woman-manly."

Genes and socialization push all of us toward either masculine or feminine inclinations. Each role carries its own blessing and curses. But together the two offer a harmonic balance, capitalizing on virtues and overcoming vices of each.

For example, Phil Jackson considers his integration of masculinity and femininity a major factor in his coaching success.

> I discovered I was far more effective as a coach when I balanced the masculine and feminine sides of my nature. . . . In my case, healing the split between feminine and masculine, heart and mind—as symbolized by my compassionate father and analytic mother—has been an essential part of my growth both as a coach and a human being. (1995, p. 76)

Today's organizations require a healthy degree of both com-passion and analysis. The two can coexist in a single person—or be represented in a pairing of opposites. Would the history of air travel be much different if former airline executives Burr and Lorenzo had reached a happy medium? Would Harpo Enterprises be as successful without Oprah's counterpart, Jeff Jacobs, as president of Harpo?

## A FINAL LOOK

The synergist and the androgynist sit at the top and bottom of the circle combining the best of all worlds. Let's assume the synergist began the journey from the right side of the model, its leadership side. Remember, the continuum is open ended, which means it can be approached from either side. We refer to it throughout the book as the "management-leadership continuum," but we could just as well call it the "leadership-management continuum." In fact, we believe it's easier to move from the "softer" leadership side to the "harder" management side than vice versa. Women seem to em-brace their masculine-management dimension more easily than men embrace their feminine-leadership dimension.

In *Primal Leadership*, Goleman, Boyatzis, and McKee stress that, although intelligence quotient, or IQ, is important, emotional intelligence, or EI, is more important.

> Throughout history and in cultures everywhere, the leader
> in any human group has been the one to whom others look
> for assurance and clarity when facing uncertainty or threat,
> or when there's a job to be done. The leader acts as the
> group's emotional guide. . . . Resonance [the term used to
> define this positive emotional phenomenon] comes naturally
> to emotionally intelligent leaders. (2002, pp. 5, 20)

In our model, IQ, because it encompasses the more technical func-tions of management, is reflected on the continuum's left side and EI, because it encompasses the more human functions of leadership, is reflected on the right. In effect, when you look at the continuum's left side you are observing the left side of your brain in action, and when you look at the right side you are observing the right side of your brain in action.

Regardless of where the synergist and androgynist started, both reflect the goal of learning to dance with your opposite. But how do you learn the rhythm and the steps?

## The Alchemist's Melting Pot

Like alchemists, androgynists and synergists take their stronger and weaker functions (symbolized in the alchemist's more precious and less precious metals) and fuse them, appreciating contributions both make to the alchemical process. Shakespeare seemed to recognize the value of these opposites when he said, "There is nothing either good or bad, but thinking makes it so" (*Hamlet* 2.2). In *Emotional Alchemy* (2002), Tara Bennett-Goleman employs the alchemical process as a metaphor for internal change.

Alchemists sat over their boiling pots attempting to transform lesser metals into more precious ones. The key to this Medieval "art" was the alchemist's attitude of not changing or throwing out anything, "'seeing that even the negative is part of the learning and healing'" process (p. 7).

In much the same way, you need to sit over your internal melting pot, rejecting nothing. Remember, even though you have a dominant style, be that rationalist, politicist, humanist, or culturist, you still have aspects of the remaining three. Recall Shakespeare's observation: none of them is bad, and, as the alchemist believed, none of them should be tossed aside. If you continue to mix and balance your internal pot, you, like the alchemists of old, will come out with a precious result: a balanced approach to managing and leading.

## The End Is the Beginning

As a circle, the management-leadership model symbolizes wholeness—the totality of a person's potential. When completing a circle, one ends where he or she began. Likewise, we end this book by returning to where we began: focusing on awareness. Recall the model's centerpiece—a lightbulb, symbolizing heightened consciousness. Although we favor the lightbulb, we could have chosen the sun. Just as a burning lightbulb penetrates darkness, a rising sun breaks through overhanging clouds. This process symbolizes shedding light on old mind-sets that keep us from seeing and embracing the organic wholeness of management and leadership. One writer describes the process:

> The warmth of sunlight dissolving the moisture of clouds—nature's alchemy—echoes the warm fire of mindfulness melting the emotional clouds covering our inner nature. The effects of such periods of insightful clarity may be fleeting and momentary, lasting only until the next emotional cloud forms. But rekindling this awareness again and again—bringing it to bear on these inner clouds, letting it penetrate and dissolve the haze in our minds—is the heart of practice, a practice we can learn to sustain. (Bennett-Goleman 2002, p. 7)

Recall our twelve profiles. Each needed to turn on his or her awareness, the internal lightbulb, and so can you. With your light turned on, you will experience an "Aha!" moment as you probe your past. The role your childhood—where you've been—played in the development of your dominant function will begin to emerge. Your next "Aha!" comes when your awareness penetrates your present circumstances—where you are now. Grasping the limited range of your style, when contrasted with others, will challenge you to expand. And a third "Aha!" comes when your awareness prompts you to envision your future potential—where you'd like to be.

Jimmy Valvano, the late coach of North Carolina State University's men's basketball team, was diagnosed with terminal cancer. In the latter stages of his disease, a tribute was held in his honor. In his speech, Valvano noted that dying gave you greater awareness. He said, "In your life the important thing is knowing where you are, where you've been, and where you're going." His advice is the cornerstone of this book.

# CHAPTER 8

# Epilogue

As we celebrated the turning of the millennium, we held high expectations for our lives and our institutions. Early on, however, many of our hopes were dashed. In disbelief we watched the meltdown of some of the country's largest businesses, such as Enron and WorldCom; the ethical violations of Arthur Andersen, one of the most respected U.S. accounting firms; the stock market's deep dive; the revelations of child abuse by priests in the Catholic Church; the spiraling costs and malpractice issues in the field of health care; and the growing concerns about the quality of education. It seems that, instead of hope, the new millennium brought wholesale crises among America's organizations and institutions. What's at the heart of this troubling scenario?

In our view, one of the root causes is the major imbalance between management and leadership. The opposites are not dancing, and, as a result, the system is out of whack. We seem obsessed with the assumption that better management will save the day, overlooking the fact that we are missing passion, purpose, and meaning. Only when we feel threatened as a country, when we go to war or terrorists strike on our own soil, do we pull together and deepen our commitments to cherished values and traditions. To put it bluntly, our country is currently overmanaged and underled.

Think about it. To remedy the mess in business, Congress will pass legislation to curtail the greed of CEOs and the autonomy of accounting firms. To halt the market's downward spiral, policy makers will play with interest rates and trading rules. The Church is outlining rules for exposing and punishing rogue priests. Many physicians are enrolling in MBA programs to learn how to better manage their practices. To improve schools, policy makers are legislating standards and specifying more rigorous accountability measures. Our unyielding faith in rationality, policy, and rules dictates how we respond to almost every crisis.

While our response may treat the symptoms and temporarily help people feel better, we believe this approach will hardly cure the ills our society faces. Of course, we need better management. But we also need more leaders to step forward, as Giuliani did in New York following September 11. We need leaders who know themselves and feel a genuine concern for others. We desperately need leaders who understand the role symbols play in the human experience. For the new century to fulfill our deeply held expectations, the cultures of our institutions need renovating and renewing.

The good news is that we may be getting help from new sources. As you have seen, our management-leadership continuum portrays leaders as humanists and culturists, a right-brain or feminist leaning. Fortunately, many more women are breaking the glass ceiling and taking top corporate leadership positions. A 2002 census revealed that the percentage of women occupying Fortune 500 executive positions had nearly doubled from the 1995 level of 8.7 percent. At sixty companies in 2002, one-quarter of corporate officers were female; yet at seventy-one other companies no women occupied top positions. In 1995, one woman was CEO of a Fortune 500 company; seven years later, six women were "500" CEOs—including Hewlett-Packard's Carly Fiorina, whose style appears to be more that of the rationalist than the humanist or culturist. At this rate it will take thirty-nine years for women to fill 50 percent of the Fortune 500 companies' top jobs (Jones 2002, p. B3). Was the glass ceiling really a floor? Or was it, to use Whyte's terms, the means of keeping women in the cellar of organizations?

We began this book with an analysis of airline executives—all men. Recently the statistics have begun to change. Almost 50 percent of airline employees are women, and at Southwest, where Colleen Barrett is president and COO, ten of the top twenty-four executives are women. Women are changing the way airlines do business: "Airline CEOs say that while many of their male managers have emphasized hardware and thought of their job as moving planes efficiently from place to place [management], women executives seem to understand that they are in a service business and that happy employees make for happy customers [leadership]" (Donnelly 2002, p. Y3). Donald Carty's forced resignation as CEO of American underscores the point. Carty, who followed in Crandall's footsteps, lost the trust of American unions—particularly the flight attendants—when he failed to reveal executive compensation packages prior to negotiating pay cuts with the unions.

Airlines are not the only organizations in which women are changing cultures. Family-run businesses are also experiencing women's impact. As consultant John Messervey says, "Daughters have leveled the playing field" (Hopkins 2003, p. B1). Today in nearly half of Messervey's client organizations, daughters play key roles; just two decades ago there were no daughters in such positions. Why the change? Messervey says, "There's less testosterone involved. Sometimes, sons miss the fine points" (p. B1)

More often than not, the fine points involve values, a point underscored by *Time*'s selection of recipients for its Person of the Year Award. Three female whistleblowers were honored as Persons of the Year in 2002. Cynthia Cooper, Coleen Rowley, and Sherron Watkins exposed the wrongdoings of their respective organizations: WorldCom, the FBI, and Enron.

Are women assuming the role of organizational change agent? If the state of the glass ceiling is any indication, the answer is yes. It appears to be falling at an ever-increasing rate, and women are playing a major role in its demise. Consider the world of athletics. Women are making tremendous inroads onto playing fields long dominated by men. But the momentum cannot be contained within the lines of a basketball court or the out-of-bounds markers of a golf course; it spills over to other areas of society. More and more women are assuming corporate leadership positions and, in the process, balancing the more rational approach of management.

But how long will current trends continue? History has many lessons to teach those who fail to heed this book's twin watchwords:

*awareness* and *balance*. Backwaters of corporate America are full of managers who failed to lead and leaders who failed to manage. Balancing effective leadership with effective management is the key to navigating the turbulent waters of the future, both personally and professionally.

Recall what we said in the Prologue. We described the stops and starts of our personal journeys as we struggled to learn to dance with our opposites, learning the tempo and the moves. Like most people, we tripped and fell many times. We simply were not aware of just how out of balance we were. While reading this book, you undoubtedly recalled a number of missteps you have made on your own journey. As you read about our mistakes and those of the men and women profiled, hopefully you took heart, realizing you were not alone.

A more positive and robust future for all our institutions will require a better balance between management and leadership. And this will be achieved only if we become more aware of our opposites and our options. Remember, all organizations are made up of rationalists, politicists, humanists, and culturists who need to become aware of their strengths and weaknesses and how to dance with their internal and external partners. The management-leadership model provides a mirror to help us all take our first steps. Carry it with you. As you revisit your image, do you still see the same person? Is your masculine or feminine dimension beginning to appear? Are you on the road to developing a more comprehensive approach to your management-leadership style? After all, when dancing with your opposite, it's fulfilling to experience the manager teaching the leader new steps and the leader guiding the manager to new tempos, all because their awareness of each other led them to ask the timeless question: Shall we dance?

# References

## Prologue

Bolman, L., and T. Deal. *Leading with Soul.* San Francisco: Jossey-Bass, 1995.

Bolman, L., and T. Deal. *Reframing Organizations.* San Francisco: Jossey-Bass, 1997.

Johnson, R. *We.* New York: HarperCollins, 1983.

Johnson, R. *He.* New York: HarperCollins, 1989.

Johnson, R. *She.* New York: HarperCollins, 1989.

Whyte, D. *The Heart Aroused.* New York: Currency/Doubleday, 1994.

Williams, R. "Theory A: Personifying the Management-Leadership Continuum" Ph.D. diss. Vanderbilt University, 1997.

## Chapter 1: Balancing Precision and Passion

Armour, S. "American Workers Rethink Priorities." *USA Today,* October 4, 2001, B1–B2.

Bennis, W., and J. O'Toole. "Don't Hire the Wrong CEO." *Harvard Business Review,* May–June 2000, 170–179.

Berglas, S. "The Very Real Dangers of Executive Coaching." *Harvard Business Review,* June 2002, 86–92.

Bolman, L., and T. Deal. *Reframing Organizations.* San Francisco: Jossey-Bass, 1997.

Charan, R., and G. Colvin. "Why CEOs Fail." *Fortune,* June 21, 1999, 69–78.

Crainer, S. *The Management Century.* San Francisco: Jossey-Bass, 2000.

Drucker, P. "Management's New Paradigms." *Forbes,* October 5, 1998, 152–177.

Einhorn, C. S. "There's No Magic." *Barron's,* August 28, 2000, 23–26.

Frattaroli, E. *Healing the Soul in the Age of the Brain.* New York: Viking, 2001.

Gaddis, P. O. "Business Schools: Fighting the Enemy Within." *Strategy and Business* 21(4), 2000, 51–57.

Ghoshal, S., and C. Bartlett. *The Individualized Corporation.* New York: HarperCollins, 1997.

Jackson, P. *Sacred Hoops.* New York: Hyperion, 1995.

Jones, D. "Some Say MBAs No Longer Worth Extra Cash." *USA Today,* July 22, 2002, B1.

Leonhardt, D. "Harvard Strives to Make Entrepreneurial Shift." *The Tennessean,* June 25, 2000, E1.

Pfeffer, J., and C. Fong. "The End of Business Schools? Less Success Than Meets the Eye." *Academy of Management Learning and Education* *1*(1), September 2002, 78–95.

Roberts, J. L., and E. Thomas. "Enron's Dirty Laundry." *Newsweek,* March 11, 2002, 22–28.

Schön, D. *The Reflective Practitioner.* New York: Basic Books, 1983.

Triay, V. A. *Bay of Pigs.* Gainesville: University Press of Florida, 2001.

Useem, J. "Tyrants, Statesmen, and Destroyers: A Brief History of the CEO." *Fortune,* November 18, 2002, 82–90.

Valdmanis, T., and A. Backover. "WorldCom in 'Death Spiral.'" *USA Today,* June 27, 2002, B1–B2.

Webber, A. "Learning for a Change." *Fast Company,* May 1999, 178–188.

## Chapter 2: The Management-Leadership Model

Cameron, J. *The Artist's Way.* New York: Tarcher/Putnam, 1992.

Langer, E. *Mindfulness.* Reading, Mass.: Addison-Wesley, 1990.

Maslow, A. *Motivation and Personality.* New York: Harper & Row, 1954.

Reed, D. "Why Airlines Have Trouble Turning Profit." *USA Today,* December 6, 2002, p. B3.

Von Franz, M-L. *Psychotherapy.* Boston: Shambhala, 1993.

## Chapter 3: The Rationalist

### Crandall References

Bryant, A. "American Airlines and Its Pilots Reach a Tentative Agreement." *New York Times,* March 20, 1997, A1, C21.

Labich, K. "American Takes on the World." *Fortune,* September 24, 1990, 40–44, 46, 48.

Loveman, G. *American Airlines.* Harvard Business Case 9-491-061, pp. 1–14. Boston: Harvard Business Publishing, 1992.

Ott, J., and R. E. Neidl. *Airline Odyssey: The Airline Industry's Turbulent Flight into the Future.* New York: McGraw-Hill, 1995.

Petzinger, T. J., Jr. *Hard Landing: The Epic Contest for Power and Profits That Plunged the Airlines into Chaos.* New York: Random House, 1995.

Plaskett, T. Interview with Roy Williams in Dallas, March 19, 1996.

Reed, D. *The American Eagle: The Ascent of Bob Crandall and American Airlines.* New York: St. Martin's Press, 1993.

Reed. D. Interview with Roy Williams in Fort Worth, Texas, March 20, 1996.

Rubin, D. "Bob Crandall Flies off the Handle." *Texas Monthly,* August 1993, 98–101, 114–120.

Serling, R. *Eagle: The Story of American Airlines.* New York: St. Martin's Press, 1985.

Solomon, P. Interview with Bob Crandall in the Admiral's Club at La Guardia, New York, on WGBH Boston, May 20, 1998 [Crandall's last day with American].

Solomon, S. "American Airlines: Going, Going, . . . ?" *New York Times Magazine,* sec. 6, September 5, 1993.


**Summitt References**

"The Cinderella Season: The Lady Vols Fight Back," prod. by John Alpert and Maryann De Leo. New York: DCTV, 1998, videotape.

"Have Mercy." *Reader's Digest* 156(934), February 2000, 56.

Rosenfield, J. "Why I Love Geno Auriemma Despite His Foibles." *Full Court Press: The Women's Basketball Journal,* www.fullcourt.com, October 17, 1997.

Smith, W. "Pat Summitt's Double Life." *Tennessean,* March 18, 2000a, D1.

Smith, W. "Summitt Reaches Pinnacle with Today's Induction." *Tennessean,* October 13, 2000b, C1.

Smith, W. "Summitt's Hall of Fame Enshrinement Celebrated." *Tennessean,* October 14, 2000c, C6.

Summitt, P., with S. Jenkins. *Reach for the Summit.* New York: Broadway Books, 1998.


**Nixon References**

Abrahamsen, D. *Nixon vs. Nixon: An Emotional Tragedy.* New York: Farrar, Straus, and Giroux, 1977.

Aitken, J. *Nixon: A Life.* Washington, D.C.: Regnery Publishing, 1993.

Barber, J. D. *The Presidential Character: Predicting Performance in the White House* (4th ed.). Englewood Cliffs, N.J.: Prentice Hall, 1992.

Gannon, F. "The Real Richard Nixon." Interviews with Richard Nixon, prod. by Raiford Communications, Inc. New York: Central Park Media, 1994, videotape.

Gergen, D. *Eyewitness to Power.* New York: Simon & Schuster, 2000.

Matthews, C. *Kennedy and Nixon: The Rivalry That Shaped Postwar America.* New York: Simon & Schuster, 1996.

Matthews, C. "Nixon 25 Years Later." *Hardball,* CNBC TV, August 5, 1999.

Nixon, R. M. *Six Crises.* New York: Doubleday, 1962.

Nixon, R. M. *In the Arena: A Memoir of Victory, Defeat, and Renewal.* New York: Pocket Books, 1990.

Schell, J. *The Time of Illusion.* New York: Alfred A. Knopf, 1975.

Woodward, B., and C. Bernstein. *The Final Days.* New York: Simon & Schuster, 1976.

## Chapter 4: The Politicist

Lorenzo References

Barrett, W. P. "Topgun." *Texas Monthly,* March 1987, 98–103, 185–190.

Bernstein, A. *Grounded: Frank Lorenzo and the Destruction of Eastern Airlines.* New York: Simon & Schuster, 1990.

Bernstein, A., C. Power, G. DeGeorge, T. Vogel, and E. Schine. "Back to You, Frank." *Business Week,* April 24, 1989, 24–26.

Bloomberg Business News. "U.S. May Give Lorenzo Airline a Second Chance." *New York Times,* March 30, 1994, D5.

Bryant, A. "Lorenzo Gets One More Try at This East Coast Airline." *New York Times,* October 8, 1993, D1.

Cook, J. "Lorenzo the Presumptuous." *Forbes,* October 30, 1978, 115–117.

Easterbrook, G. "Lorenzo Braves the Air Wars." *New York Times,* November 29, 1987, 17–70.

Engardio, P., J. Norman, M. Frons, and A. Bernstein. "Frank Lorenzo, High Flier." *Business Week,* March 10, 1986, 104–107.

Ennis, M. "Sky King." *Business Month,* September 1988, 27–34.

Moritz, C., ed. "Frank Lorenzo." In *Current Biography Yearbook,* 367–371. New York: H. W. Wilson, 1987.

Murphy, M. E. *The Airline That Pride Almost Bought: The Struggle to Take Over Continental Airlines.* New York: Franklin Watts, 1986.

O'Brian, B. "For Lorenzo Getting a New Airline Aloft Is Proving Treacherous." *Wall Street Journal,* January 25, 1994, A1.

Ott, J. "Lorenzo-Led Team Bets on Friendship Airlines." *Aviation Week and Space Technology,* April 12, 1993, 32–33.

Passell, P. "Judging Lorenzo: Air Regulators Are Where They Didn't Want to Be." *New York Times,* September 16, 1993, D2.

Petzinger, T. J., Jr. *Hard Landing: The Epic Contest for Power and Profits That Plunged the Airlines into Chaos.* New York: Random House, 1995.

Pfeffer, J. *Managing with Power.* Boston: Harvard Business School Press, 1994.

Plaskett, T. Interview with Roy Williams, Dallas, March 19, 1996.

Schwartz, J., E. Calonius, D. L. Gonzalez, and F. Gibney Jr. "A Boss They Love to Hate." *Newsweek,* March 20, 1989, 20–24.


**Clinton References**

Alinsky, S. D. *Rules for Radicals.* New York: Random House, 1971.

Bennet, J. "The Next Clinton." *New York Times Magazine,* May 30, 1999, 26.

Clinton, H. *Living History.* New York: Simon & Schuster, 2003.

"Hillary Clinton for the Senate." *New York Times,* October 22, 2000, sec. 4, 14.

"Hillary Rodham Clinton: Changing the Rules." *A&E Biography,* #AAE-10431, prod. by ABC News, exec. prod. Robert Roy, 1994.

Kiely, K. "Hillary Clinton Building Legacy of Her Own." *USA Today,* July 10, 2001, A8.

Maraniss, D. *First in His Class.* New York: Simon & Schuster, 1995.

Maraniss, D. *The Clinton Enigma.* New York: Simon & Schuster, 1998.

Noonan, P. *The Case Against Hillary Clinton.* New York: Regan Books, 2000.

Olson, B. *Hell to Pay: The Unfolding Story of Hillary Rodham Clinton.* Washington, D.C.: Regnery Publishing, 1999.

Safire, W. "Blizzard of Lies." *Time,* January 8, 1996, 27.

Sheehy, G. *Hillary's Choice.* New York: Random House, 1999.

Sheehy, G. "Hillary's Solo Act." *Vanity Fair,* August 2001, 130–135, 177–182.

Simpson, C. Interview with Bill Clinton, "This Week," ABC, November 14, 1999.

Walsh, K. "Portrait of a Marriage." *U.S. News and World Report,* August 31, 1998, 27–31.


**Johnson References**

Barber, J. D. *The Presidential Character: Predicting Performance in the White House.* Englewood Cliffs, N.J.: Prentice Hall, 1992.

Caro, R. *Master of the Senate.* New York: Alfred A. Knopf, 2002.

Kearns, D. *Lyndon Johnson and the American Dream.* New York: Harper & Row, 1976.

"LBJ." *The American Experience,* PBS, A KERA production in association with David Grubin Productions, Inc. North Texas Public Broadcasting, 1991, videotape.

Stahl, L. "The LBJ Tapes." *60 Minutes,* November 11, 2001.

## Chapter 5: The Humanist
Burr References

Aronoff, C. E., and J. L. Ward. *Donald C. Burr, Contemporary Entrepreneur.* Detroit: Omnigraphics, 1992.

Barrett, A. "The Last Romantic." *Financial World,* May 14, 1991, 50, 51.

Booker, B., et. al. *People Express: A Leadership Plan for Donald Burr.* MBA class project, Owen Business School, Vanderbilt University, 1996.

Byrne, J. A. "Lofty Ideals and Firmly Planted Feet." *Business Week,* November 25, 1985, 80–94.

"Decline of People Express." Harvard Business School video #890-508. Boston: Harvard Business Publishing, November 10, 1988.

"Donald Burr: Question and Answer Session with an MBA Class." Harvard Business School video #885-516. Boston: Harvard Business Publishing, July 15, 1985.

Gendron, G. "Bitter Victories." *Inc.,* August 1985, 25–35.

Glassman, J. K. "Aarant Burr." *New Republic,* October 6, 1986, 11–13.

Holland, P., and M. Beer. "People Express Airlines: Rise and Fall." Harvard Business Case #9-490-012. Boston: Harvard Business Publishing, 1990, revised September 4, 1993.

"People Express Philosophy: Interview with Prof. Michael Beer." Harvard Business School video #890-507. Boston: Harvard Business Publishing, November 10, 1988.

Petzinger, T. J., Jr. *Hard Landing: The Epic Contest for Power and Profits That Plunged the Airlines into Chaos.* New York: Random House, 1995.

Plaskett, T. Interview with Roy Williams, Dallas. March 19, 1996.

Prokesch, S. "Behind People Express's Fall: An Offbeat Managerial Style." *New York Times,* September 23, 1986, sec. 1, 1; sec. 4, 8.

Ramsey, D. K. "Dogfight over Deregulation." In *The Corporate Warriors,* 140–175. Boston: Houghton Mifflin, 1987.

Rhodes, L. "That Daring Young Man and His Flying Machines." *Inc.,* January 1984, 42–52.

Rimer, S. "The Airline That Shook the Industry." *New York Times Magazine,* December 23, 1984, 24–30.

Whitestone, D., and L. A. Schlesinger. "People Express." Harvard Business Case #9-483-103. Boston: Harvard Business Publishing, 1983, revised May 10, 1995.

**Friedan References**

Friedan, B. *The Feminine Mystique.* New York: W. W. Norton, 1963.

Friedan, B. "Woman: The Fourth Dimension." *Ladies' Home Journal* 81 (5), June 1964, 12, 47–55.

Friedan, B. *Life So Far.* New York: Simon & Schuster, 2000.

**Carter References**

Barber, J. D. *The Presidential Character: Predicting Performance in the White House.* Englewood Cliffs, N.J.: Prentice Hall, 1992.

Brinkley, D. *The Unfinished Presidency: Jimmy Carter's Journey Beyond the White House.* New York: Viking, 1998.

Carter, J. *Why Not the Best?* Nashville: Broadman, 1975.

Carter, J. *Keeping Faith: Memoirs of a President.* New York: Bantam, 1982.

Carter, J. *An Hour Before Daylight.* New York: Simon & Schuster, 2001.

Fallows, J. "The Passionless Presidency: The Trouble with Jimmy Carter's Administration." *Atlantic,* May 1979, 33–48.

"Jimmy Carter: To the White House and Beyond." A&E *Biography,* #AAE-10495, prod. by ABC News, exec. prod. Lisa Zeff, 1995.

Johnson, H. *In the Absence of Power.* New York: Viking, 1980.

Mazlish, B., and E. Diamond. *Jimmy Carter: A Character Portrait.* New York: Simon & Schuster, 1979.

Mihalec, J. "Hair on the President's Chest." *Wall Street Journal,* May 11, 1984, 30.

"Voice for Peace." *Atlanta Journal-Constitution,* October 12, 2002, A1, A10–12.

Young, A. "Former President's Award Long Overdue." *Atlanta Journal-Constitution,* October 12, 2002, A11.

Zoroya, G. "A Day in the Life of America's Plainspoken Man of Peace." *USA Today,* October 14, 2002, D4.

## Chapter 6: The Culturist

**Kelleher References**

Brinkley, D. Interview with Herb Kelleher on "This Week with David Brinkley," July 18, 1993.

Butler, C. "Herb, the Love Bug." *Incentive,* November 1993, 52, 53.

Chakravarty, S. N. "Hit 'em Hardest with the Mostest." *Forbes,* September 16, 1991, 48–51.

Engler, A. "A Busy Boss Can Never Fly Solo." *Business Month,* August 1990, 22–23.

Fisher, A. B. "Where Companies Rank in Their Own Industries." *Fortune,* March 4, 1996, F1, F2, F6.

"Getting High on Love and Laughter." *Reputation Management,* July/August 1995, 61–66.

"Gimme Five." Southwest Airlines video, 1996.

Gross, T. S. *Positively Outrageous Service and Showmanship: Industrial Strength Fun Makes Sales Sizzle.* New York: Mastermedia, 1993.

"Herb Kelleher Speaks on Leadership." Southwest Airlines video, n.d.

"Heroes of the Heart." Southwest Airlines video, n.d.

Jarboe, J. "A Boy and His Airline." *Texas Monthly,* April 1989, 17, 98–103, 140–144, 153–155.

"Just Plane Fun Shuffle." Southwest Airlines video, n.d.

Keel, B. Interview with Roy Williams, Nashville, Tennessee, January 27, 1996a.

Keel, B. "Just Plane Wild." *Business Nashville,* March/April 1996b.

Kelleher, H. Press conference at the Nashville Airport, February 26, 1996a.

Kelleher, H. Speech given at the Nashville Rotary Club, February 26, 1996b.

Kelleher, H. Speech given at Mayor's Workshop, Nashville Civic Center, April 2, 1997.

Levering, R., and M. Moskositz. *The 100 Best Companies to Work for in America.* New York: Penguin, 1993.

Lewis, J. Interviews with Roy Williams, Nashville, spring 1994–summer 1996.

"Luv Story." *Spirit* (Southwest Airlines magazine), June 1996. Jonesboro, Arkansas: AA Inflight Media.

"Malice in Dallas." Southwest Airlines video, n.d.

McCartney, S. "Airline Industry's Top-Ranked Woman Keeps Southwest's Small-Fry Spirit Alive." *Wall Street Journal,* November 30, 1995.

"Morris Airlines Wedding." Southwest Airlines video, n.d.

*Our Colorful Leaders.* Southwest Airlines publication, 1996.

Owen, K. Spirit: *Transformation and Development in Organizations.* Potomac: Abbott, 1987.

Personal observations by Roy Williams: Trip to Southwest Airlines corporate headquarters, March 18–21, 1996; Southwest Airline flights 11 and 1039 on March 21, 1996; Southwest's Nashville Station ten-year party, March 18, 1996, at the Nashville Airport; Southwest's twenty-five-year celebration, June 18, 1996, at the Nashville Airport.

Petzinger, T. J., Jr. *Hard Landing: The Epic Contest for Power and Profits That Plunged the Airlines into Chaos.* New York: Random House, 1995.

Southwest Airlines. Annual Report 1995.

Southwest Airlines Culture Day, Southwest Airlines corporate headquarters, Dallas, September 20, 1996. (Conference of international managers and leaders.)

"The Tale of Two Men, One Airline, and a Cocktail Napkin." Southwest Airlines publication, 1996.

Southwest Airlines. "Our Colorful Leaders." Southwest Airlines publication, 1996.

Stein, N. "America's Most Admired Companies." *Fortune,* March 3. 2003, 81–89.

Stewart, E. Interview with author, Dallas, Texas, March 20, 1996.

Tenney, D., and M. Smith. "Kelleher Builds Southwest Success with 737s." *Professional Pilot,* March 1990, 48–51.

Turner, M., and C. Newsom. "Herb Kelleher on Life and Success." *Professional Review,* fall 1994, 45–48.


**Oprah References**

Chin, P., and C. Cheakalos. "Touched by an Oprah." *People,* December 20, 1999, 112–122.

Clemetson, L. "Oprah on Oprah." *Newsweek,* January 8, 2001, 38–48.

Donahue, D. "Live Your Best Life, with Oprah." *USA Today,* July 2, 2001, D1–D2.

Donahue, D. "Hooked on Classics, Oprah Revives Book Club." *USA Today,* February 27, 2003, D1.

Harrison, B. "The Importance of Being Oprah." *New York Times Magazine,* June 11, 1989, 130.

Lowe, J. *Oprah Winfrey Speaks.* New York: John Wiley and Sons, 1998.

Mair, G. *Oprah Winfrey: The Real Story.* Secaucus, N.J.: Citadel, 1994.

Sellers, P. "The Business of Being Oprah." *Fortune,* May 6, 2002, 50–64.

Winfrey, O. "Become More of Who You Are." *O,* May–June 2000, 57.

Winfrey, O. "What I Know for Sure." *O,* July 2001, 194.

**Reagan References**

Barber, J. D. *The Presidential Character: Predicting Performance in the White House.* 4th ed. Englewood Cliffs, N.J.: Prentice Hall, 1992.

Bosch, A. *Reagan: An American Story.* New York: TV Books, 1998.

Cannon, L. *Reagan.* New York: Putnam, 1982.

Cannon, L. *The Role of A Lifetime.* New York: Simon & Schuster, 1991.

"Carter-Reagan Presidential Debate," October 28, 1980, Cleveland, Ohio, moderator Howard K. Smith. Commission on Presidential Debates, www.debates.org.

Dallek, R. *Ronald Reagan: The Politics of Symbolism.* Cambridge: Harvard University Press, 1984.

Matthews, C. *Hardball,* CNBC TV, March 11, 1999.

McFeaters, A. "After 10 Years, Reagan Is a Strong Political Buzzword." *The Tennessean,* February 7, 1999, D6.

Noonan, P.. *When Character Was King.* New York: Viking, 2001.

Reagan, R., with R. G. Huber. *Where's the Rest of Me?* New York: Karz-Segil, 1965.

Reagan, R. *An American Life.* New York: Simon & Schuster, 1990.

Reagan, R. *A Shining City: The Legacy of Ronald Reagan.* New York: Simon & Schuster, 1998.

"Ronald Reagan: The Role of a Lifetime." A&E Biography, #AAE-14095, prod. by ABC News, exec. prod. Josh Howard, 1998.

Sperber, M. *Onward to Victory: The Crisis That Shaped College Sports.* New York: Henry Holt, 1998

**Chapter 7: Reflecting While Dancing**

Bennett-Goleman, T. *Emotional Alchemy.* New York: Three Rivers Press, 2002.

Brady, E. "Time Fails to Lessen Title IX Furor." *USA Today,* June 19, 2002, C1–C2.

Gavora, J. *Tilting the Playing Field: Schools, Sports, Sex, and Title IX.* San Francisco: Encounter Books, 2002.

Goleman, D. R., Boyatzis, and A. McKee. *Primal Leadership.* Boston: Harvard Business School Press, 2002.

Jackson, P. *Sacred Hoops.* New York: Hyperion, 1995.

James, W. *The Varieties of Religious Experience.* New York: Triumph Books, 1902.

Johnson, R. *Owning Your Own Shadow.* San Francisco: Harper Collins, 1991.

Woolf, V. *A Room of One's Own.* New York: Harcourt Brace, 1929.

## Chapter 8: Epilogue

Donnelly, S. "The Sky's the Limit." *Time,* July 15, 2002, Y1–Y7.

Hopkins, J. "More Daughters Get Keys to Family Firms." *USA Today,* January 6, 2003, B1.

Jones, D. "Women Gain Corporate Slots." *USA Today,* November 19, 2003, B3.

# Index